AN EMPOWERED *Life*

Aldwyn Altuney
Christine Innes
Jenell Kelly
Kleo Merrick
Kylie James

Lisa Ohtaras
Marika Gare
Terri Tonkin
Tracey Korman
Vallye Adams

The Corporate Escapists

Copyright © 2022 by Christine Innes

All rights reserved. No part of this book may be reproduced in any form on or by an electronic or mechanical means, including information storage and retrieval systems, without permission in writing from the publisher, except by a reviewer who may quote brief passages in a review.

This book is designed to provide information and inspiration to our readers. It is sold with the understanding that the publisher is not engaged to render any professional advice. The content of each month is the sole expression and opinion of its author and not necessarily that of the publisher. No warranties or guarantees are expressed or implied by the publishers' choice to include any of the content in this book. Neither the publisher nor the author(s) shall be liable for any physical, psychological, emotional, financial, or commercial damages including, but not limited to, special, incidental, consequential or other damages.

First printed 2022 by The Corporate Escapists.

Printed on-demand in Australia, United States and the United Kingdom.

Table of Contents

Introduction — v

Christine Innes — 2
A new beginning

Jenell Kelly — 16
The greatest lie I ever told myself was that I had competition

Terri Tonkin — 30
It is your choice, to choose your life

Marika Gare — 40
An empowered life

Kleo Merrick — 54
The definition of empowerment

Vallye Adams — 66
Helping the helpers

Kylie James — 84
Standing at a crossroads

Lisa Ohtaras — 96
Change your thoughts change your life

Aldwyn Altuney — 110
From depressed & suicidal to inspiring truth & good news

Tracey Korman — 126
How I healed my life for my son

Authors Biographies — 143

Introduction

We never know the impact that one's story will have on another person. It can change their entire life. I know the effect that stories have as they changed my life. I went from being broke, broken, leaving a toxic and unfixable marriage, and filing for bankruptcy to creating the life and business of my dreams... all from the power of stories.

When life was giving me more than a few lemons, I would read books, and watch snippets on YouTube of people who have changed their life. It was stories that gave me the courage to not only change my life, but it would also allow me to share my story in a way that would give me the power back to take control of my life.

The impact one's story has is immense and the stories in this book have the power to change lives.

These incredible, powerful, and inspirational women all have shared their stories to inspire you. I know that from reading these stories, you will feel inspired to take action and be inspired that you can make the changes needed to be happy, joyful, loved, and follow your passion.

Change is difficult, it pushes us outside of our comfort zone. I know that change can be hard yet rewarding. I encourage you, after reading this book to make one change. That one change will cause a beautiful ripple effect in your life and then come back and read the book again and implement another change and keep doing this over and over again.

I never liked the saying when I was younger "If I can do it, you can too". I was this overweight kid watching the toned girls in their bright leotards exercising and repeating that phrase over and over again. Yet here I am at 45 saying this now to you "If I can do it, you can too".

Stepping every day into the unknown and trying different practices each day allowed me to change my life. It is hard work every day, however, I choose when I wake up each day to be happy, to step into gratitude, and live An Empowered Life. That each day is filled with love, joy, happiness, gratitude, and fun.

I wish this for everyone on the planet and to know how it can feel to live An Empowered Life.

Take this book and use it as a handbook to inspire you to take great action toward your own Empowered Life.

I can not wait to hear all about it.

Love and light

x *Christine*

CHAPTER 1

Christine Innes

A new beginning

"DREAMS + ACTION = REALITY"
~ Christine Innes

It was an illusion

I am trying to get up from the chair to make my way to speak to an audience to share my own story. I felt the nerves set in, the discomfort all over my body, and the inner critic in me was getting louder and louder.

That mean girl voice inside of me was telling me all the things I have been thinking.

Who do you think you are?

Seriously, who wants to listen to you?

Is it because of all of your mistakes you are here?

Just a fat girl trying to make something work!

That voice was loud today and as I was walking up to speak, I thought I needed to cut her off or it will be over before I start.

I took a deep breath and remembered my WHY. My own purpose I am here for.

It was starting to work, yet the whole speech is a blur. I don't remember anything!

All that night all I could think about and kept asking myself "Was this an illusion, was I actually there?"

I had been in a place of sleepwalking through life before and I thought I had made a conscious effort to be present, yet the old pattern and behavior were starting to creep back in.

I wasn't prepared for things to go back to how they were a few years ago. I needed to settle in to be uncomfortable and look at why this was all happening again.

Starting over again

It was time to be uncomfortable. I had been playing it safe now and well, the universe and myself are telling me to stop - step up - and reset.

I know the events that got me to play safe. In February 2022, another relationship ended. It hit me hard and I did not see it coming. I was comfortable in life, I was happy, I was safe.

AN EMPOWERED *Life*

So why??? All the questions came pouring out. Why did this end? Why me? Why now? Why can't I make this work?

Most of the time we need reflection to see the WHY. To be able to see the events for the gifts they are giving you.

It is hard when your heart is breaking and you are trying to figure life, business, and everything out in between.

It was a few months after the breakup when I walked onto the stage to speak to a live audience and this time gave me the change of perspective I needed.

The why was getting softer and I was seeing that it wasn't just about me, it was about my purpose, my vision, and also other people in my life.

Now to be clear, this has taken years of internal work to slowly see the reflection of my higher self to be able to help come to this realisation.

The ability to know and yet also understand that nothing is happening to you, it is happening for you. When I first heard this I laughed so hard as all I wanted to do was sit in the "Poor Me" state and have what I call a pity party.

With all the internal work I have been doing, I knew it was time to start over. To take a deeper look and focus on the future. The past is there as a reminder but not for me to stay there and wallow.

It is time to allow the new vision to come to life and reset, realign and refocus on my passion and drive for life and my business.

Reset, realign, refocus

It had been a crazy few months, learning to adjust to being alone. To get back to focusing on myself and my goals. I learned that in all of my relationships one key factor is that I lose myself.

I put everyone else first, including their goals, their dreams, and their own wants and needs.

So it was time for me to get back into the driver's seat and set a new destination for myself.

This was the reset time.

Where did I want to go?

What did I want my life to look like?

All of these questions kept coming up and I knew exactly how to get the answers.

It probably was the first time in a few years that I could go back to my own learning and reapply them.

To find out the WHY, I sat and meditated and started my visualisation of seeing myself happy, content, and motivated.

I used a practice called "An Ideal Day". Nothing like groundhog day. It is a day that you can have on repeat, a day that inspires you to be the best version of yourself, where you are surrounded by people you love, you are inspired, lit up, and following your dreams and passion.

I found a quiet space and got to work on creating my own Ideal Day.

As I closed my eyes and connected to my own heart, my own feelings, and desires, I gave myself permission to be in the creative moment.

I started with how I wanted to feel when I woke up in the morning, I put all my feelings into the process and wanted to ensure I felt all the emotions. As I leaned into the process more, I could begin to feel the touch of the sheets as I stretched out in the morning, with the rays of sunlight beaming through my window, and the best part was I was waking up in my own bed.

I can smell the salt air and get up and walk along the beach each day with my puppy.

As the "Ideal Day" started to unfold the key message was that I was comfortable with being by myself.

The first time in over 7 years.

This was the REALIGNMENT I needed.

To see myself as happy, safe, and secure by myself.

The refocus is the hard part. As you can have all the nice dreams and goals but to refocus is the ACTION.

How can I get to this part? What is the action I need to take?

Taking action

Just as I thought I was ready to go and start my life again by myself, I was hit with another hurdle.

My dad had been sick for a few years and in August this year (2022) we were told he would need to move to palliative care. The time we have to spend with him is precious.

After my breakup, as I do, I moved back to my parent's place. I am so fortunate to have them and be supportive as this is my safe place to regroup.

As I was preparing to leave, my inner voice told me to stay.

A lot of people don't get precious time with a loved one in the last months, weeks, and days and I can see the fortune of this moment to have this time.

My action from my own reset, realign and refocus is now in a different place.

I used again, my own learnings to help me deal with the action and to deal with grief, and most of all, the uncertainty of life.

Seeing someone deteriorate and become dependent on others hits you hard.

My dad is the backbone of our family. He is more than a dad, he is also the first man I learned to trust and love. He is our life coach, business coach, handyman, joker, and singer, and he helped me raise my own son.

The action for me was to find the balance between the life I have seen in my "Ideal Day" and the life I am facing NOW and how to merge the two together.

The different pathway

Merging reality and a dream together is a delicate process.

I want to go full steam ahead of making my dream a reality however dealing with watching my Dad slowly decline, I now need to make the transition gradual.

AN EMPOWERED *Life*

So how does one do this without going crazy, I hear you ask. Great question and now it is definitely time for me to pull out everything I have learned over the past five years of my own personal development.

The first part is to give myself some grace.

The time to grieve when I feel the emotions overcome me.

As I am writing this, my Dad is still with us. I have learned a process of grieving while they are here so I can also be fully present with him. It is called Anticipatory Grief. You are watching a loved one slowly pass away and allowing all the emotions to surface and process.

As a spiritual person, I am also seeing this as a way for me to be present at the time when he does pass away and as the oldest child, be there for my Mum, my siblings, and my son.

To do this I have surrendered to the following.

1. To be kind to myself every day
2. To take the actions I can - reasonable actions to continue to work on my dream.
3. When working on my business, to be fully present and focused on the key task.
4. To be fully present when spending time with my Dad. To spend the quality time I need to make a bank of memories to help me when the time comes to say goodbye.

The new way

When I started on my spiritual journey five years ago, the biggest light bulb moment was when I was taught - "It is not happening to you, it is happening for you".

This key phrase is what I am leaning into every day now. It is not about what is happening to me, but what can I learn from this.

The breakup, the re-adjusting to being alone, the change in my business, the change in my own personal circumstances, the change in seeing my Dad decline, and knowing that we have weeks left with him.

What can I learn from this?

What is going to be my own biggest challenge?

What is going to be my own takeaway and realignment in life?

Over the past few weeks, I have already learned that I have so much strength, resilience, compassion, and resourcefulness.

Learning how to deal with and process my own grief and how I can assist others deal with theirs.

Learning that I can rely on myself and trust my own intuition.

The most surprising thing is that during all the chaos and changes my own trust and faith in myself is strong. I know that the "Ideal Day" I can see is coming. I know that the strength I have in myself is also being used for my family. I know that the vision, the goals the plans I have for my business, are all coming together.

AN EMPOWERED *Life*

What is keeping my faith is the three key principles I use in life.

The Three Key Principles in Life

When I started sharing my story over five years ago and then built a business around it, I realised I had based this on three principles.

The three key principles I have created are:

1. **Dream** - Create your own ideal day
2. **Values** - Find out what you stand for, because if you stand for anything you will fall for everything
3. **Your future self** - Look forward to your own future self. Only glance back to see how far you have come.

I live and breathe by these principles every day

Let's talk about values. Your core values are your foundation for life. They are what grounds you, they show you are a person and what you stand for..

Values are something you should be proud of, willing to scream them from the rooftops proudly. I spent a lot of time working on my own values and integrating them into my life.

Here are my own top 10 values: I live and breathe by these and I know you will be able to see how I am able to stay focused on my goals and allow the precious time with my Dad and my family.

1. **Love** - Even when I feel the fear and the self-doubt creep in, I lean into love..especially leaning into loving myself even more. To this day, I am still learning this

and learning to love my flaws as well. This is not about ego, it is showing kindness to yourself and also allowing yourself to see the beauty in yourself and others

2. **Trust** - Learning to trust myself, my decisions, and trusting others. It is about trusting the process, which is a major part of the Law of Attraction - as the universe has your back.
3. **Faith** - Having the faith within myself that I can achieve my goals
4. **Authenticity** - Always be ME! No more pretending and hiding behind a suit of armor. Simply be me as I am enough
5. **Family** - Family comes first
6. **Integrity** - always show up every day as my true self and be consistent in my thoughts and behaviours.
7. **Fun** - Have more and more fun every day. The more fun I have, the more success I have in my life and my business
8. **Dream** - Don't stop dreaming. I allow myself to be creative and bring on those big dreams and goals for myself.
9. **Loyalty** - Be loyal to myself and others
10. **Freedom** - Give myself permission to be the person I choose to be and without judgement of myself and towards others.

Creating your life

Imagine for a moment you could honestly say that you had a life that was filled with love, joy, abundance, and happiness.

AN EMPOWERED *Life*

How would that make you feel?

How tall would you be standing?

How proud would you be?

I can honestly say I have all of this in my life and I feel amazing and blessed,I walk with my head held high and I feel so proud of myself that I have created this.

I am surrounded by loving, beautiful, and inspiring people, I am lit up and I am creating my own happiness and opportunities that bring me joy.

None of this would have been possible without having made the decision to change my life and to give myself permission to change.

I can admit that for most of my life I sat in what I call the "victim mindset". You know, the poor me, feel sorry for me, help me - yet do it for me. When everything in my life was crumbling, I am pretty sure I said all those and much more.

I was having a pity party for myself. You know those parties where you sit and feel sorry for yourself, wallow, eat junk food, cry, and can't see the light at the end of the tunnel.

When I stopped having the victim mindset, I switched my mindset to see things as learning lessons, and not just that it was happening to me, it was happening for me.

Let me say that again

It was not happening <u>to</u> me, it was happening <u>for</u> me

This powerful sentence can change the way you view all obstacles you face. It gives you a different perspective and shifts you into a more positive mindset.

Now I see the difficult times in my life as a blessing. These challenges have made me into the person I am today and have given me the opportunity to create the life I have today. I would not change any of it.

When you are standing at a crossroad in your life, you are always being given an opportunity. These choices give you the opportunity to either see the decision as an obstacle or as a lesson in life.

For me, I will always choose the lesson and see it as something I need to learn from as it allows me to continue to grow as a person.

Allowing magic in

Knowing what I know now, I appreciate all the moments in life. The good, the not-so-good, and all the stuff in between.

I am truly grateful for all that I have and excited about what is ahead for my business and my ability to process the emotions to deal with my Dad and grieving.

One key message I keep on getting from the universe is....

NEVER UNDERESTIMATE YOUR POWER!

Everyone has magic inside of them and I know I have been able to harness that magic and help others by following my Three Key Principles.

Allow yourself to be, and access your insights into the life you want to create, a life where you can be back in the driver's seat and set the destination of your own choice.

I know that if I can do it, you can too

AN EMPOWERED *Life*

The golden key to remember is to have fun, have trust and faith within yourself, and remember you are worthy enough to achieve your goals.

With this, you can achieve anything.

Love and light

x Christine

Power Summary

Let's do a quick recap of the Three Key Principles:

1. Dream - Create your own ideal day
2. Values - Find out what you stand for because if you don't stand for anything you will fall for everything
3. Your future self - Look forward to your own future self. Only glance back to see how far you have come

Success actions

Here are Three Success Actions that you can do right now to make a big impact in your life.

1. Give yourself permission to have FUN!
2. Give yourself permission to DREAM!
3. Give yourself permission to BE YOU!

Jenell Kelly

Leadership Success Trainer, Amazon #1 International Best-Selling Author, Keynote Speaker, and Certified Clarity Catalyst Coach, USA.

CHAPTER 2

Jenell Kelly

The greatest lie I ever told myself was that I had competition

---

Like many others, as a young child, I had a very vivid and creative imagination. Our big yellow home sat at the end of Sycamore Avenue in the suburbs of Philadelphia. It was surrounded by woods and the muddy brown river where the trees became my playground. Playing outside was my favorite childhood pastime, you could barely get me to come in the house even after dark. On sizzling summer days, I would run through the yard in my bare feet feeling the warmth of the sun beating down on my golden blonde hair while the coolness of the green grass squished between my little toes. In those moments, I remember the feeling of freedom as the wind brushed across my face and my muscles hurt from the ongoing belly laughs while my friends and I played through the day. During the winter months, when the weather was too brutal for outdoor play, I looked forward to preparing for the holidays! Spending hours in the kitchen with my mother, mixing bowls and cookie sheets scattered about the room and the aroma of freshly baked cookies coming from the oven. We baked cookies by the dozens! I didn't realize, as a child, that it was my mother's side hustle! I had red and green sugar sprinkles everywhere and enough chocolate chips in my tummy for five kids! Baking and decorating, along with crafts and painting were a few of my favorite creative outlets.

My younger years were not always rainbows and butterflies. Raised in a lower middle-class household, having financial challenges, wearing secondhand clothing, and both parents working full-time hours created an environment of stress for all involved. My father, having earned a Purple Heart in the Vietnam War was a hero, yet suffered the consequences that showed up as Post-Traumatic Stress Disorder (PTSD). It was never spoken about. As a child, I was not aware of the effect my environment would have on my life or the amount of healing that would later be required for me to achieve elevated levels of success. The moments of chaos and disconnect and feelings of abandonment turned out to be exactly what was needed for me to share my unique gifts with the world. God / Universe / Spirit (whichever you prefer) had a perfect plan!

We have all experienced pain to a degree in our lives whether it occurred as an innocent child from well-meaning or not-so-well-meaning people that cared for us or as we blossomed into young adults and experienced our first heartbreak, physical trauma, or major loss. The levels and degrees vary greatly but what remains similar is that when pain is managed rightly it produces invaluable gifts such as strength, endurance, compassion, and empathy. Most would agree that their greatest gifts and triumphs have stemmed from some of their most challenging moments.

It was July 10th, 2011, when I awoke in my ICU bed post-surgery from a catastrophic injury to my lower spine. Listening to the beeping of alarms and the shuffling of feet from nurses hustling by, I peeped open my eyes to see the unsettled look on my mother's face. Slowly, as I started to gain more consciousness, I glanced around the room noticing pumps, cords, monitors, and drains hanging over the bedside. My mouth felt so dry like I was harvesting a field of cotton balls in it. I could feel the crisp hospital air and the warmth of my mother's hand holding mine but sensed immediately that something was off. The surgery was intended to bring back the feeling and mobility in my left leg, not leave me numb from the waist down. At this moment, like every moment in our lives, I had a choice to make. I could panic, become fearful, and doubt or I could simply be present and trust everything will work out as planned.

My ten-year recovery was one of divine design. Each physical step represented the pathway to empowerment. Each breakdown built my mental character. Every setback elevated me spiritually and guided me to my current realm. The first three years stripped me of everything on every level; my career, my income, my home, my peace. My dignity disappeared during my bankruptcy and foreclosure, and I was handed forms that labeled me "disabled" by Insurance Physicians who never once spoke to me. As a nurse of many years, I had well-meaning people in my corner, but we did not share the same vision for my future. To this day, those first few years of recovery remain the greatest test to my commitment of will and my belief in powers greater than myself.

To have a vision is not as profound as having a vision tied to unwavering belief. Believing in your ability to bring your vision forth in the world as a materialized object or way of being is where your power lies. You see, I did not lay numb on a hospital bed, "convincing" myself that I was going to fully recover; I had unwavering certainty. I lived in that certainty with every breath I took, every word I spoke, and every thought I created. It did not matter that top Surgeons, Physicians, or Physical Therapists told me otherwise. It did not matter the amount of excruciating pain I endured, the sleepless nights, the intense burning, and spasms. It did not matter that I was labeled, "disabled", and further payment was denied for physical therapy. Or that it cost me the roof over my head and every dollar of my life savings. It did not matter that I was never officially, "medically cleared", to return to work. Nor did it matter that I would have random falls that resulted in needing two more surgeries down the road. None of it was relevant! So often people give up on their dreams and simply hand their power and in turn their life over to other people's thoughts and beliefs. My example may seem extreme and untypical but where in your life do you choose to stop? At what moment does doubt kick in for you?

I have found having belief can be one of the greatest challenges along our path of empowerment. Too often we look at our current circumstances and think things are not possible. When we set off on what is referred to as "The Hero's Journey", a journey to create change in our life, we will be faced with challenges. The Hero's Journey, a six-stage process that requires patience and determination. Stage 1 starts with a calling, an "ah-ha" moment that something in our life requires change. Stage 1 is referred to as the "Preparation Phase" which is your initial confidence and vision. In this stage, it seems doable to get from point A to point B. For the Entrepreneur, it is that initial thought of wanting to start a business, to break free from the constraints of their "9 to 5" or to help solve a problem in the world. You feel the initial rush of adrenaline, the fired up, lit up, unicorn dust feeling on the inside. You plug into trainings, attend calls and gather necessary tools. You set out to "do the do" only to realize you are not having the level of success you thought you would. You start to feel frustrated, and you question whether it is for you. You compare your beginning to other people's endgame and every single self-limiting belief starts to rear its ugly head! The inner voice is telling you that you are not good enough, you are not smart enough, you aren't meant for this, and the list goes on and on. It is at this moment when you have entered Stage 2 of your journey, you have so gracefully crashed into the brick wall of frustration! Welcome friend. This stage is where those with grit, determination, and tenacity stick around and where most of the world walks away letting their dreams and extraordinary life die! The elite group of individuals who stick around on their path start to let go of the judgment, quiet the self-limiting beliefs and be open to knowing it is ok to let their idea percolate while they temporarily focus elsewhere to aid in finding solutions. They look for allies and search for resources as they trust in themselves to move forward. This temporary "backburner" situation is Stage 3 referred to as "Incubation," mixed with Stage 4 "Strategizing." If you make it this far along the journey, you have started to build your belief!

Success does not happen overnight; it happens in stages one step at a time. There is no straight line from point A to point B. One day you awaken with excitement and a feeling of obviousness! Your solution feels like it came out of nowhere, this is Stage 5, the stage of "Illumination." Although it feels as if your solution was an overnight thought, it was the result of preparation and strategy. And the final and most fulfilling stage is that of "Verification," bringing your creation out into the world and achieving your desired result in life. This moment requires massive amounts of celebration!

Our power lies in having a deeper knowledge of how life works, the various stages of our personal and professional journeys. Knowing that frustration and feeling stuck are key players in the process of creation should empower you to never give up on your goals, your visions, or dreams and to just keep going.

Judge and be judged

"Why do you look at the speck of sawdust in your brother's eye and pay no attention to the plank in your own eye?" -Mathew 7

I reached a point in my physical healing where I returned to working at the hospital. The first few years I never shared with my co-workers my physical struggles'. To outsiders, my life looked well put together. I had an extremely fulfilling career in the healthcare field and was a leader in the industry. I traveled several times a year, always surrounded by friends. I wore nice clothes and drove a nice car. What was not visible to the outside world in addition to the internal physical pain was my sense of loneliness, feeling as if I never quite fit in, of not being enough which led me to be a people pleaser. I couldn't fully express myself and constantly had a deep longing for something more than what currently was.

I spent from age 17 to 47 placing others' needs in front of my own, caring for the elderly, the debilitated, and the traumatically injured. Mourning death and celebrating life with only moments in between did not allow for proper grieving or emotional expression. The field of ER / Trauma Nursing can be described as organized chaos; always waiting for the other foot to drop! For many years, I loved that organized chaos, the buzzing energy that filled the department, the emotional roller coaster, the loud sounds, and the camaraderie amongst the staff - until the day I no longer did. It was a typical Wednesday afternoon listening to the hustle and bustle of the ER. I could hear the alarms of the monitors going off to the left and the right. The sound of the EMTs chatting with the patients as they pushed them down the hall and in the far distance, I could hear Fire Rescue calling in a trauma alert. Then suddenly, it was as if time stood still and all the years of suppressed emotions, all the days of putting others' needs in front of my own, all the times I was made to feel as if my efforts weren't enough, washed over me like a huge wave crashing upon the shore. I could feel it deep inside my body as I heard a voice inside my head say, "I don't want to do this anymore." At that moment I felt fear, overwhelmed, confused, and I felt lost. I have done this my whole life. I paused, took a deep breath and I assured myself that something will come along, that it would work out because it always does. The next two years were brutal to my heart and soul. I was trying to serve from an empty cup but my cup was not only empty it was broken into jagged edge pieces all over the ground.

We create thoughts and opinions about other people's lives based on their outer appearances, their status in the workplace, the car they drive, the clothing they wear, and the amount of money we think they have. But mostly we judge ourselves. We compare ourselves to others and use that comparison to measure our level of success and worthiness. And what we see in others, good or bad, often reflects how we feel about ourselves. Judgment can be detrimental to self-growth. We miss opportunities and connections that are right in front of us because they do not show up in the "packaging" we were expecting.

Jenell Kelly

Consciousness and experiencing your experiences

One of the greatest gifts I received as I moved along my journey from ER nurse to entrepreneur was the gift of consciousness. It was a long and winding road with many turns and speed bumps but the depth of gratitude I have for each experience, each layer peeled away, every step taken, and every conversation spoken is as vast as the universe will allow. Along my journey, all my self-limiting beliefs took center stage! My ego was challenged and fought back like a warrior defending his Kingdom. The energetic and emotional sensation that occurred as I left my old ways of being and entered a new world was a slow resistant pull. Imagine yourself at the bottom of a pit of quicksand and swimming your way to the top. The light above was not visible, but I knew it was there. It took great strength to propel myself upward especially when every fiber of my being wanted to stop. It was a heavy load to carry but as I shed my self-made armor piece by piece from around my heart, and placed it lovingly beside me, the weight of the load lessened. I am in gratitude for my armor because it protected me for many years, it created comfort as I fulfilled my assignment as a caregiver. Without it, I would not have been able to endure others' pain and suffering. Releasing the armor and lessening the weight allowed me to move gracefully upward towards the light. This in turn solidified my trust in what I was reaching for.

To break through, we must first be willing to break down, look inside and face our shadow selves. They are the parts of us we keep hidden from the rest of the world. Much like the armor I removed, I feel deep gratitude for the shadows inside of me. My shadows are a huge contribution to where I am now in my life. Also, I am grateful beyond measure for my ego, all of my self-doubts, and the feelings of not being good enough, not pretty enough, not smart enough, all of them! They kept me grounded and got me exactly where I am today. And, knowing that the ego is not going away, not while I'm here on this earth, I've learned tools and techniques that allow me to love and quiet it. To not allow it to grab the steering wheel of my vehicle called life and drive me in directions that no longer serve me. Until you have this awareness you will find yourself making U-turns, driving in circles, or moving so slowly that you do not get anywhere.

My journey to consciousness was a cocktail of confusion mixed with excitement and a burning desire to keep going no matter what showed up along the path. You cannot rush it or bulldoze your way through in doing so you will just repeat the lessons you missed. You will experience many interactions, conversations, experiences, and emotions. Be sure to pause and ask yourself questions such as "Why is this showing up in my life?" and "What is this here to teach me?" Take time to experience your experience without getting caught up in it. Some people spend decades in situations that do not serve them because they allow their emotions to drive their vehicle. Whether it is a person, a relationship, or a situation, seek to understand why it showed up and learn from it without allowing your emotions to keep you stuck there.

Everything is a choice. You may not realize it at first, and you may not agree with it, but when we stand in it our power is palpable. When in every moment we say to ourselves, "I have a choice at this moment" we tap into our greatest self. There is nothing less empowering than feeling as if you are a victim of a circumstance, keeping your opinions and your thoughts to yourself, or being told how you feel is silly or stupid. All too often we feel tied down by our current reality, we allow the amount in our bank account, our living situation, or our level of education to hold power over us. You no longer need to operate from outside circumstances.

As newborns we arrived here perfect, whole, and complete, we did not arrive here "not enough." And we most definitely did not arrive here unlovable and unworthy. So, what changed? As children, we have experiences and interactions that shape our inner world. For example, a 6-year-old child may experience the loss of a parent through divorce or separation. In their 6-year-old mind, they make up that their parent left because they were unlovable and not enough. The truth is their parent leaving was a neutral situation. Having the ability to look at all situations as neutral and knowing the only "charge" they have is based on the story we make up about them is very empowering. Understandably, a 6-year-old child would tell themselves that their parent leaving meant they are unlovable. But as the child tells themselves this story over and over it becomes part of their belief system. Beliefs are just thoughts we think over and over until they become part of our subconscious mind. So, the unlovable 6-year-old little girl or boy becomes the unlovable teenager who becomes the unlovable young adult who becomes the unlovable middle-aged person. And, when we don't feel lovable, we don't feel enough, and it reflects in every area and situation in our lives. The belief that supported the 6-year-old child in their moment of pain does not support a grown adult. It leaves the adult walking around the world feeling hurt, feeling like a victim, feeling not enough, unworthy, etc. It is a deep story that gets to be acknowledged and healed to create differently moving forward.

Since everything in our life is attached to our worthiness, being willing to do the inner work, to go into the shadow sides of our soul, and heal our hurt inner child is extremely valuable. It takes courage, strength, grit, determination, love, grace, and compassion. It is as hard, or as easy, as we make it, and it is a choice. God did not bring you here to play small. He brought you here as a beautiful, loving, extraordinary individual with unique gifts and talents to share with the world. You are not ordinary; you are not here to be part of the faceless crowds or nameless souls with no honor or dignity. You are extraordinary! And you were born to be a changemaker in the world.

When you are willing to release yourself-made armor and drop from your head to your heart, you will find hidden treasures of untapped potential and priceless pieces of yourself waiting to be born. Time is ticking, it's time to drop the bad habits, and discipline your life, every detail. It's time to come alive! Release judgment, let go of expectations, listen before you act, treat yourself with grace, have patience, and allow love to fill every cell of your body. When you start to realize that everything in the world was created from nothing, you'll start to realize you can create anything you desire. This is no easy feat without having blind faith in something greater than yourself. Be open to breaking down so you can experience the emotions, learn the lessons, clean it up without dwelling on it, and move forward.

Your assignment

It is in the process of falling deeply and divinely in love with oneself, in love with God, that our true calling unfolds with clarity. There will be times when your assignment requires you to elevate to levels of selflessness you never knew existed to serve your purpose. It's a BIG ask. This does not mean you place others' needs in front of your own, or that you work endlessly and tirelessly to the point of exhaustion. It simply means you recognize the difference between love and ego. When you live to serve you accept that there are no mistakes in your connections.

Each interaction is divine, and when managed appropriately it is a win/win for all parties involved. At times there will be joy, happiness, and laughter along the way, those are the times that immediately light us up inside! Then there are times when the hardest decision to make is the right decision. It is preceded by feelings of sadness, grief, unfairness, etc., it's what makes it a BIG ask. There is great power in being committed to your calling. Grace, love, and forgiveness are key players. Not only for ourselves but for those we encounter along the way. You must be willing to let go of what anyone else thinks of you, your journey is not theirs. And anyone on their true path never judges another, they simply recognize and support the divine work at hand. Trust that nothing meant for you can be taken from you and that everything is always working out for you even in moments of despair. Especially in the moments of despair.

Everything in life is a choice. Where are you choosing comfort over commitment? The need to be right over love? The willingness to settle over moving into the unknown? Ego over God? Start asking yourself these questions, because we are not here to simply slide by in life, we came here to be extraordinary. Do you know what your purpose is? Do you value yourself enough to care? When you do, you will live a life of empowerment.

CHAPTER 3

Terri Tonkin

It is your choice, to choose your life

"What you do makes a difference, and you have to decide what kind of difference you want to make."
~ Jane Goodall

Empower. Empowered. Empowerment.

In recent years, these words have become like buzz words, particularly when talking about women, and what they can do. For some, it may mean being in control, taking consistent action, or knowing where you are headed. For others, these words can bring on anxiety and overwhelm, as some people are not sure what is expected of them. This can become an issue, as I believe, we do not have to live up to the expectations of others. Definitely set your own standards and expectations for your own life. Do not let others impose their expectations of how they believe you should live your life. Let others live their life the way they want to, and you live yours.

For me, being empowered means I am in charge of my choices. And those choices can be across all elements and aspects of my life. I get to choose what food I will eat, or not. I am able to choose if and when I will exercise. I even get to choose what work I will undertake, and work I will say no to.

This is my life. Why shouldn't I get to make those choices?

There is a caveat here. You have the right to make your own choices, absolutely. When you make your choices, you have to own it, accept and take responsibility for those choices, and the consequences of those choices, both positive and negative. They are your choices, from start to finish.

I have been fortunate throughout my life, and grateful for the opportunities I have had, through work, travel and relationships. My parents were hard-working individuals, who always ensured my brothers and I had everything we needed. We didn't always get what we wanted, yet my parents did the best they could, with what they had. The things we wanted would come by way of birthday and Christmas presents. We learnt to appreciate these things and to be grateful for receiving them.

As children, we were encouraged to try new things. My brothers knew how to cook, do the washing and how to iron their shirts. I did too, of course. I was taught how to work the garden, mow the lawns, and work on engines. So did my brothers. We all got to go fishing, gem hunting and camping. We learnt many things by observing and then doing. One of my brothers, and

I, have always loved reading. My other brother loved to rescue injured birds and animals.

Our education wasn't only delivered to us by sitting in a classroom at school. My dad was practical and shared his skills and wisdom. My mum was nurturing and encouraging. Education was important to both of my parents, as they had grown up during the depression years. They believed education was the gift that keeps on giving, as it would allow us to follow our dreams, to become what we wanted to become, and to have the knowledge to learn the skills we would need.

My dad would encourage us all to develop our own skill sets, including using our mind. He would ask us what we thought about different topics and to share our opinions. The best thing was, we didn't have to agree with him. Regardless of what our opinion may have been, he would always ask us why, or how we had come up with that opinion. He didn't want us to agree with everything we heard, or saw. He wanted us to develop the skills we would need as we got older, to hold our own in the presence of others, respectfully. Not to be nasty or mean, yet be able to have constructive conversations.

When I left school, I had a number of options available to me. I was accepted into Special Education Teachers College, I had passed the exams for the Commonwealth Bank, National Bank and the state public service; and I had passed the necessary testing for the Women's Royal Australian Air Force (WRAAF). I even had an offer of full-time employment with a film laboratory where I had been working over the Christmas period.

Choices.

I spoke with my parents, as I had only turned 18 shortly after finishing school, about all the options. We looked at the pros and cons of each, what opportunities I could have, and I had to consider moving away from home especially for the WRAAF. There was no guarantee I would stay in Brisbane with the other choices either, however it was more likely I would.

I was the baby of the family, and the only girl. What was the best option for me.?

My parents told me to follow my heart. Not as easy as it sounds. Since I was little, I had always wanted to be a teacher. I had the opportunity right in front of me, ready for the taking. At 18, in that moment, it wasn't the most appealing. I decided, to join the WRAAF.

After three years and seven months, I made the decision to discharge from the RAAF, as the WRAAF had integrated into the RAAF. Back then, it wasn't easy for a married woman to progress through the ranks, as we were limited if our husbands were in a similar mustering (work/job). My career was also limiting my husband's career. When I discharged, he was posted to a new locality and promoted. It was the way it was.

We decided we would start our family and I would return to the workforce at a later time. I actually got a position when we arrived at our new location, and they asked me if we were going to have children. This would not be allowed today. However, I said no, no plans for having children at this stage. The universe had different ideas. I fell pregnant within a few months. OOPS! We had two sons, three years apart, before being on the move again. On our next posting, I commenced working in the banking industry. I held many positions with the bank, from teller, customer service office, overseas officer, training, supervisor to branch accountant. I always put my hand up for any personal or professional development opportunities. It was the best way to keep learning. After 14 years, I chose to take a redundancy.

AN EMPOWERED *Life*

I moved into youth work, assisting students transition from school to further education, training or employment. This was one of the best jobs I have ever had. Watching young people light up as they were guided and encouraged to have belief in themselves. The outcomes achieved through the program had ripple effects for years.

From there, I moved into the public service, where I was contract managing the youth programs I had recently left. Having worked as a practitioner, I understood the challenges organisations faced when working with young people, especially if they had disengaged from education. It wasn't always easy to bring them back into a learning or employment environment, as their belief in themselves was pretty low. I was able to work with the organisation staff to develop strategies appropriate for young people to re-engage in learning, either through training or employment.

After I left the public service, I needed time for myself. The work environment had become toxic, as it was during a time of massive, and constant change. People were overwhelmed and scared of the future. I chose to take a redundancy, to escape the toxicity.

I didn't want to be with people. I wanted to curl up with a good book, and let the world go by. So, I did. For almost a year. When I felt well enough to venture out, I did some volunteering at the local neighbourhood centre helping with literacy and numeracy, and at my grandson's school for assisted reading. It was as much as I could do for some time.

I've always enjoyed personal and professional development, and was the first to put my hand up if there were learning opportunities in any and all of my employment roles. I had been interested in life coaching for some time, and had even started a course many years previously. I had done the basic introduction weekend, NLP (Neuro Linguistic Programming), and Masters NLP. However, for many reasons, I had not followed through with it.

I saw an opportunity to attend an introduction to life coaching weekend, with a different organisation to the one I had been with previously. I decided to attend, to see if my interest was still there, and if so, where this could take me.

It was a two-day event, Saturday and Sunday. Off I went on the Saturday morning, and I fell back in love with coaching. My love of PD kicked in and I was hooked again. I phoned my hubby and said "Guess What!". His reply, "You're going to do another course, aren't you?" He knew me well.

I told him the cost of the investment, we discussed it, and I signed up. This time I completed the course. I started my business, did some coaching, and ran some workshops. Within six months of starting my course, my mum was moved into care. She became my priority.

I kept my business going, slowly. I started my own meetup group, developed and facilitated a wonderful group of women. I completed my studies. I wrote and published my first book, as I wanted my mum to read it before she passed away. (Writing a book had been another childhood dream). It was beautiful when I gave her a copy of my book, and even though she was suffering from dementia, she remembered I had always wanted to write a book, when I was a little girl.

When mum passed away, I stepped right back from everything. I needed time and space to grieve, and to decide what was best for me. After some months, I decided I would kick off again, only to be hit with my husband being made redundant unexpectedly, and in the following month, the pandemic virus turned the whole world upside down. As my husband had been planning to retire later the same year, we decided we would both retire and travel. Obviously, that didn't happen. We had to cancel all of our travel plans.

So, what to do?

I was fortunate to have a number of writing opportunities as a contributor to some compilation books come my way, and I jumped at it. Since the pandemic hit, I have contributed to eleven compilation books (many are International Best Sellers), and have been a regular contributor to an online magazine.

I have extended my writing to provide services to those wishing to write a book, yet for many reasons are unable to do so themselves. Now, I am not only an author with my own book and several compilation books, I am also a ghost writer. I have completed a number of manuscripts for my clients, I have been approached to write for a web designer and to write some blogs for a travel agent.

Since moving into ghost writing, I have been asked many times if I do copywriting. It was not something I had considered; however, I am now expanding my writing services further and considering copywriting and content writing. I help other writers by doing deep dive beta reads, offering suggestions for improvement and formatting. I believe I have found my passion, writing.

Throughout my life, I have learnt a lot about myself. Who I am, and am not; my beliefs; my values; my strengths and my weaknesses. I know what brings me joy, I know what work I like to do and enjoy.

As much as I would like to think I am perfect, I know I am not. I do know, I am imperfectly perfect, or perfectly imperfect. Either way, I have my flaws. We all do, and that is okay.

Having studied and worked in the coaching space, I am fully aware of limiting beliefs, reframes and comfort zones. I have seen many coaches try to 'fix' their clients. Nobody needs fixing. We are not broken. We have flaws, some of which need some TLC (tender loving care). I have done a lot of work on myself over the years, and have been coached by others.

I know there are things I cannot do, and there are things I have no desire to do. At times, I love living in my comfort zone. I am quite productive when I'm there. I have stepped out of this zone many times, and at other times, I have stepped firmly into this zone. Both of these situations work well for me. I have lived experience of both.

With all due respect to coaches, please do not tell me I have limiting beliefs and I can change them. Please, do not tell me to get out of my comfort zone, as that is the only time I will grow. Please do not reframe what I say, and please do not try to fix me, as I am not broken.

For anyone who is a coach, has a coach or is wanting a coach, this is my experience. Coaches are important people we need to have in our lives. Everyone should have at least one coach in their lifetime, and maybe one for each different area of your life. This is up to you. They can see things we cannot see; they hear things we do not say, they can guide us, they can nurture us and they will ensure we get the outcomes we are seeking.

This is how I am empowered, and what empowerment means for me. I accept and acknowledge it is different for each of us.

AN EMPOWERED *Life*

I know my strengths, and I work to continually improve them. I know my weaknesses, and I know when to walk away from things when it is not working for me. I will find a way, my way, where I am able to use my strengths to achieve the result I want, or need.

Do I do life on my own? No, I don't. Do I live my life on my terms? Yes, I do.

As I said previously, my parents were wonderful teachers, guides and nurturers.

I have been fortunate, some may say lucky, to have been with my husband for coming up to fifty years. We have two adult sons and five grandchildren. We were both in the Defence Forces (RAAF) and moved around for twenty years. It wasn't easy, new jobs for me, new schools for the boys, making new friends, finding a new doctor or dentist, and everything else that goes on with removals.

I have met many wonderful people in my travels, and each one has provided me with insight and taught me lessons.

All of my experiences, the good, the bad and the ugly, have taught me what I needed to know. Every experience provides a lesson. Each person you meet, comes into your life for reason, a season or a lifetime.

One of my mantras is – everything happens for a reason, good or bad, learn the lesson and improve the outcome.

> "You were put on this earth to achieve
> your greatest self, to live out your
> purpose, and to do it courageously."
> ~ Steve Maraboli

Marika Gare

International best-selling author, International multi-award winner, Business Operational Management Specialist, Mentor, founder and Director of Perth Virtual Services and Women's Circle Facilitator, Australia.

CHAPTER 4

Marika Gare

An empowered life

I dedicate this chapter to my son Joey; he lights up my world every moment of every day. May he always know his true worth, follow his own inner compass and have the courage to be true to himself. Love you always and forever, to the moon and back.

"Living an empowered life means living life for you and being true to yourself no matter how hard it might be. Loving yourself wholeheartedly and being confident enough in yourself to live the life you want and of which you have always dreamed."

Empowerment means so many things to so many people....

To me as a woman, empowerment comes in the form of knowledge, control in your choices and life, and the ability to know your self-worth, who you are on a soul level, and the spiritual journey you are on. It is never holding back from what you want, being bold and courageous, and always following your heart and dreams.

Essentially, it is being true to yourself, loving yourself first above all else, and knowing your worth.

What I have learned in life is that most of us just want to be happy. Really, truly happy. But many of us have had experiences in our life that can be painful and so we have a choice about how we navigate through these, how we reflect back on these memories, and choose what we are going to keep alive and what we are going to release.

As we age and experience the complexities of life, relationships, traumas, death, and everything in between, we often become disempowered through our own ideals or views of ourselves brought on by these experiences. It may start in childhood with bullying or lack of parental connection or develop as we get older and endure toxic relationships or difficult friendships, and we slowly lose confidence in ourselves and who we are.

This lack of confidence and desire to please others and be accepted makes us lose our true selves as we become victims of our own choices, not wanting to change or move forward in case it all goes wrong and it becomes too hard. What if I really stuff up? What if I lose everything? What if nobody likes me and I end up all alone?

AN EMPOWERED *Life*

And yes, there is safety and enjoyment in living a 'safe' life, but we are often left dreaming of bigger and better things, of excitement and spontaneity and freedom and true enjoyment for our soul. At least that is how I felt...

Life does not always go to plan, but it is through the rubble of despair that we grow, inspire, and become the beautiful, flourishing souls we were meant to be.

Becoming aware

Empowerment is awareness of self and of the mind – how you see yourself, how you view others, how you perceive situations (negative or positive), how you view your journey in life (victim or warrior), and how well you know yourself and your triggers, how to navigate through difficult times, health conditions or traumatic memories...and most of all... the confidence you have in yourself and the courage to be bold, to be who you are regardless of what others think and be audacious in your ambitions, have pure determination and motivation to get what you want out of life. Choose to love, choose to follow your dream, and choose yourself above all else.

Because why not? What is holding you back? The only thing that disempowers us is our own minds and how we perceive ourselves and the world around us. Each and every moment we experience, we make choices, and they are not always going to be the right choices and that's ok. It is how it is meant to be so we can learn and grow and become stronger and more determined for what we truly want and deserve in life.

The higher powers that be have a plan and I believe our souls choose our life before we are born so all that happens and all that is, is how it is meant to be and is what has been chosen for our soul's development and for our journey in this lifetime. If it were not for the events and experiences we have endured, we would not be where we are today, we would not grow to be strong warriors of our own destiny and courageously audacious human beings.

Becoming aware of your path and allowing your inner guidance to guide you through and provide insight and clarity to situations and challenges, brings great joy and potent potential.

It starts with me

During my life, I have endured many challenging situations which have led me down my own road to self-empowerment. It is through these challenges that I have learned the pathway and tools to empower myself and to be able to guide and empower others.

One of these challenging situations was enduring a major car accident in 2013 where I was forced to build myself again from the ground up. Literally.

Prior to the accident, I was a workaholic working two jobs 7 days a week, day and night running my hobby business in between, saving for a house with a man I did not truly love and who didn't truly love me, and I'd lost track of my true self and my purpose. I thought it was what I wanted but looking back I knew it was not right for me, but I continued on the course anyway to avoid difficult decisions and being on my own. There was safety in my choices, but not happiness.

So, the universe said, nope, time to teach you the way again – you are destined for greater things in this life, you have lost your way and I am going to reboot you, change everything in your life so you can start again, regain the love of self and life and be the warrior you were born to be. And in time, you will share your wisdom with others who are suffering. And that's my real life's purpose – to help others heal, to reignite them with their beautiful selves, and show them the road home.

It is funny how going through so much pain and devastation makes you so much stronger and happier than before because you appreciate every little thing and see the world through a clearer and more beautiful lens.

So, 2013 was the year I had my major car accident in the middle of a jungle no less, in Thailand. The driver was showing off and being reckless with his driving and lost control. We were on a dirt road that backed onto a cliff face that went a looooooong way down. We hit a tree at about 80km p/hour and ended up rolling 6 or 7 times. During the accident, I hit my head with such force that it cracked my skull between my eye sockets, and I was knocked unconscious for around 45 minutes and they could not wake me. I suffered internal injuries and bruising, a torn spleen, several deep lacerations to my face resulting in emergency plastic facial surgery, and obtained severe brain trauma. I lost 70% of my memory, I lost physical and cognitive functions, and it took a year and a half of physical rehab and 3 years of constant brain training and development to get back to my full capacity. It was a long road….

As you can imagine, losing so much of your memory means losing a large part of who you are. Our memories are what form us, are where we learn and grow and develop who we are, so I spent a long time feeling very lost and confused. I mean I knew who I was, but I had lost those memories and experiences that formed who I was over my lifetime. Losing brain function and abilities was also very frightening because I was an intelligent woman. Before the accident, I had the memory of an elephant and prided myself in the knowledge of many things. I was nicknamed the Oracle at work because of my wealth of knowledge. Then in the blink of an eye, I lost all of that and I could not even remember how old I was, let alone talk properly.

I had forgotten people's names, family members, and people and friends I had known for years, I lost the ability to speak properly, and my brain would muddle up my thought process. For example, I would go to say to someone "Hi how are you going?" But my mouth would say "going hi ya." And each time I tried to correct myself it would just come out more jumbled. It was not matching what my brain was thinking and it was extremely frightening and went on for many months after the initial accident as my brain was severely swollen and bruised and not able to function properly. I suffered nightmares, reliving the accident over and over again every night for months, and had intense anxiety and PTSD. Some days just the thought of leaving the house was too much for me and I would break down in tears after spending hours trying to build myself up just to walk out the door.

But I was not going to be defeated, I did not want to stay like that forever, I wanted my life back, and I hated feeling scared and anxious all the time. So I worked hard every day to train my brain to function back again and regain my memory. I used meditation to find my calm and make sense of the dreams and scattered bits of memories I started getting back, trying to find who I really was again. It did not always make sense, but I wanted control of my mind again.

So I focused on what I remembered, how I remembered feeling with each memory and really drew out information from it like what people and places were in my life at that point and what they were like. I trained myself to really focus on each memory with intensity until I remembered every aspect of it. Or at least most of it.

Each time I got new information from my brain I really absorbed it. I started a journal of how I was feeling and the growing memories, and although I still felt really confused a lot of the time, I came up with a plan of what I wanted in my future so I could visualise and focus and use it as motivation on my really tough days where I sat and cried for hours at what I had lost. I did puzzles, I looked at photos, and I spent all my time training my brain back and encouraging my inner self to guide me through. There is such self-awareness during these times and all I wanted was to fix myself, fix my brain and then fix my life to be the best life of my dreams.

Unfortunately while recovering from my accident, there were other challenges placed in my way (you know, just to make sure!). Six months after the accident, I discovered my partner of 12 years had been 'finding love elsewhere' would be the best way to put it. We were in the process of buying a house and trying for children (which was put on hold after the accident until I'd recovered) so this absolutely shattered me as you can imagine. I had put so much into this relationship and got nothing in return. I packed up my belongings and walked out with not much more than the clothes on my back. I just wanted out and to start afresh with a new life. After the struggles I had been through I just wanted to be happy.

A month later I met a man that seemed very supportive and loving initially and I wanted to immerse myself in something new to take my mind away from everything else, and I was lonely, so I just went with the flow to see where it would all take me. It moved very quickly and before long we were living together.

But as I would soon find out this man I initially thought was a nice person would quickly turn into a very controlling and very violent abuser who took whatever was left of my soul and crushed it. I was obviously still recovering physically, mentally, and emotionally from my accident and long-term relationship breakdown so was I very vulnerable to this behavior.

Stepping into my own empowerment

Being in a very violent relationship was where I felt all my empowerment was taken from me and I realised what I wanted seemed even further from reach, but I was ready to fight for it. Fight even harder and stronger than before.

But then, just to throw more on top, my father was diagnosed with his second very aggressive brain tumour. The doctors basically said to say our goodbyes now because even though they planned to operate, the chances of survival were extremely low. And if he did survive, he would most likely have severe physical and mental disabilities. Things would never be the same. My father is my rock and the thought of having our relationship cut short was incredibly difficult to get my head around, but I also needed to be strong for him and it was time for me to be his rock and support him through what was an even more challenging time for him. How do you say goodbye and prepare for the worst but be supportive and encouraging at the same time?

So, I had a multitude of challenges in my midst, and it forced me to really fight even more for what I believed, what I wanted, and to grow, develop and empower myself again. Not just for me but for my family.

AN EMPOWERED *Life*

It was time to step into my own empowerment and begin my life again.

The healing begins

When I escaped my DV relationship literally with my life, I reconnected with where I had left off before all this happened. I never in my wildest dreams thought I would end up where I had been and for anyone who understands what this is like, either severe brain trauma or DV, it really is like living in hell and every single day is a struggle to think straight and you are just focused on survival.

Anyway, I began mediation again and centered myself on healing from the inside out. I was like a battered lion, still with some fight left, but physically, emotionally, and spiritually exhausted, covered in scars and a shell of my former self.

I forgave myself for the situations I had found myself in because they were not all my fault and I know I deserved a good life with love and happiness and all the beautiful things I had been envisioning. I wanted to empower myself again, it was time to move on from these unfortunate events and gain my power back. Have confidence in myself again and move forward.

So, I made a vision board and wrote down a 5-year plan – I wanted to buy my first home, I wanted a loving relationship, to have children, I wanted my own business, I wanted to travel, and I wanted to enjoy each, and every moment life has to offer, never forgetting what I felt like at that moment. To build wonderful, loving friendships and share all life has to offer with those I love.

5 years later I had done all these things I had set out to do and had dreamed of on those dark days. I empowered myself through

self-awareness, self-training, and personal development. I gained as much knowledge as possible about anything and everything I had an interest in, and I set my intentions and goals. I never lost sight of the prize. I wanted what I wanted, and nothing would stop me. I had pure determination and a rock hard plan in place.

When you make the conscious decision to empower yourself, the world is your oyster, you are ready to bloom, and the universe will support you on this path. Nothing can stop you.

Intuition and a focused mind are very powerful things and with harnessed focus, you can change anything – your pain, your heart rate, your sense of self, your moods, your health – anything. Your whole body can go into fight or flight mode just over a memory or a thought of something traumatic, and it has been proven through research that constant stress and negative thoughts can lead to severe illness and even disease so it is only natural that it can have the same effect in the opposite direction.

I am not saying empowerment is about being bubbly and an insanely positive person all the time where everything is perfect, and nothing will ever bother you. Life will always have its challenges and we must honour ourselves and feel all the emotions along the way, even the difficult and sad ones, but we must also forgive ourselves and those that may have caused destruction in our lives because this is also what shapes us and gives us the strength, motivation and the determination to succeed in life and empower ourselves. We are all on our own journey.

AN EMPOWERED *Life*

Follow your own empowerment and guidance

Empowerment to me comes from our inner guidance and intuition, our subconscious thoughts, and how we perceive and react to all that is around us. This is relative to our physical health, and also our mental and spiritual health. The way we think of ourselves, our past, our situations, triggers, experiences and how we see others, their involvement and how it has affected us, how we observe situations and our mindset, and how determined and confident we are, all determine how we react and navigate through situations and challenges throughout life now and in the future. If you have confidence in yourself, who you are, what you want, what your worth is, and what you deserve combined with insightful observation, you can achieve anything.

Most of us see the world through a series of filters and when you tap into your inner guidance through meditation and reflection, the veil lifts and you see the true perspective. Memories are constructed in the brain with reduced consciousness, so it allows us to see the foundations of its construction in our thought process and perception, giving us the ability to reprocess in a more understanding and loving way, empowering us to move forward and live our true best life through higher knowledge and understanding.

Coming into your own power, harnessing what is available to you, and starting the meaningful change and transition into healing yourself and harnessing your own strength and power is a very dynamic tool.

By choosing positive thought processes, designing our thinking and mindset, and utilising meditation, we can heal ourselves, ignite our inner bank of knowledge and enable a better state of being.

To live an empowered life....

Tools for empowerment

Here are some tools to help guide you towards EMPOWERING YOUR LIFE:

1. **NEVER FORGET WHO YOU ARE**

    You know, the young child that was full of brave insightful awareness, who spoke their truth and had audaciously wonderful dreams. Remember that child within you and bring that enjoyment for life back, in all its tenacity.

2. **KNOW YOUR WORTH**

    Acknowledge all the weird and wonderful parts of you and know that you are precious. What you bring to the table and what you offer as a human being is worthy of great things and accept nothing less. Don't allow anyone to treat you less than you deserve or think they are better than you for any reason. Because they're not. Nobody is better than anybody on this planet, we're all equal, we are just different from each other and that's what makes life interesting. It doesn't make us less or better than anyone else, just different. Find your tribe, follow your own path, love yourself above all else, and love the life you live.

3. **GUIDE YOURSELF WITH INNER KNOWLEDGE**

    Connect to your inner higher self and obtain the knowledge and guidance that is there to bring your audacious dreams to full reality. Honour your inner wisdom and insightfulness and be the power of your own destiny.

AN EMPOWERED *Life*

4. **FORGIVE YOURSELF**

   For any choices or situations in life that could have been better. We do the best we can do at each moment in life and that's all we can do. Allowing yourself to forgive past actions or emotions and release these is empowering you to move on. It is what it is, and we always learn from our journey. Take the positives out of each situation and use them to grow.

5. **BE AUDACIOUS AND COURAGEOUS IN ALL YOU DO**

   If you really want to live your best life, do it! Work towards creating what you want, in business, in life, as a partner, as a friend, in any situation. Be audacious, go get what you want out of life and empower yourself to be happy every single day.

What are the characteristics of an empowered woman?

An empowered woman is a seeker. She takes steps to discover her life purpose and dedicates herself to living in a way that aligns with it. She knows that living her purpose will bring meaning and fulfillment to her own life while improving the lives of those around her.

CHAPTER 5

Kleo Merrick

The definition of empowerment

To those souls needing the occasional reminder of how bold and sassy they truly are.

I used to think that empowerment was something lost that you had to find. Like an old book or a piece of jewellery that has been misplaced. That when you needed it and I mean really needed it, it would just show up. Like a switch, you can turn it on or off.

Gurus like Tony Robbins, in strong husky voices, would shout out – "you need to feel empowered", or "empowerment is a mindset". And even though he's most probably right, how do you get to that point? That's a great destination, but how do you get there?

In short, how do you feel empowered?

Well firstly, what is empowerment? According to the Oxford Dictionary, there are two meanings and even though they may seem similar at first, they are vastly different.

Empowerment (Noun)

1. Authority or power given to someone to do something.

2. The process of becoming stronger and more confident, especially in controlling one's life and claiming one's rights.

Can you see the difference?

No?

That's ok, you're not alone, I didn't see it either, at first. Let me explain.

Definition one

The first definition is what Tony Robbins is talking about and even though he means well with his messages, this is how most people process and come to understand the meaning of the word. Read it again.

The authority or power **'GIVEN'** to someone to do something.

There, it is. Can you see it now?

Most of us believe that we must wait for someone or something completely external to us, to **'GIVE'** us Empowerment. As if it would magically find us, anoint us with 'empowerment' and then we can go on our merry way.

It's like waiting to be knighted by the 'Empowerment Sword' before going on the quest to slay our mighty dragons or challenges if you will.

It's a lie.

We've all been waiting for it to just turn up. I know this because I've been hunting for the *magical anointment* and the *empowerment sword* for 43 years – and it does not exist.

I believe we've all been looking and waiting for this to happen to us. Instead of making it happen for us. And in the meantime, have been hiding out from our awesomeness because we've been waiting for someone or something to 'give' it to us.

But here's the kicker…

We don't even realise that this is what we're doing. And we are very good at disguising this in other forms, such as procrastination, overwhelm, perfectionism, indecision, anxiety, or stress.

Or not having the right template, the right course, or the right mentor, coach, or support system. And even when we have all those things, we still stop ourselves from moving forward, whilst we sit and wait… for the Anointed Sword of Empowerment.

And either consciously or unconsciously, on some level, we willingly give away our power and render ourselves helpless to the situation.

Maybe we read the wrong definition? Let's try the second one instead.

Definition two

'The **'PROCESS'** of becoming stronger and more confident, especially in controlling one's life and claiming one's rights.'

There it is – Process!

That brilliant word that no one wants to hear, because of the time, hard work and pain associated with it. This one needs the wood gathered, the fires stoked, and the boilers to boil, to begin the slow and steady churn of the engine. And this must happen before we hope to accomplish anything.

In the words of Gurus like Zig Ziglar, Ralph Waldo Emerson, and Gabrielle Bernstein, who have all said, "It's about the journey, not the destination".

Simply put. It! Takes! Time!

We all **WANT** Empowerment, but we all **NEED** the Process.

So, the solution is now simple. We all **WANT** the Anointed Sword of Empowerment, but we all **NEED** the engine. So, let's start gathering the wood and stoke the fires! What are we waiting for?

And if we are all searching for the same thing, let's work together. Hooray!

You grab that branch and I'll start cutting down this one so we can chuck it in the fire. Let's get those gears moving, come on! This is gonna be awesome!

Wait, where did everyone go?

Oh, I see, you don't want to build the fire together. You want to build your own fire.

Ok, that's fair, I guess. How come?

Oh, because it might get too big too quickly? And the engine would go too fast and then lead to overwhelm, procrastination, perfectionism, indecision, anxiety, or stress? Or not having the right template, the right course, or the right mentor, coach, or support system?

Well, shit!

Now what?

What went wrong? Maybe we looked at the wrong dictionary or something?

Or could it be, that in our search for the meaning of Empowerment all our fears welled up inside us, completely unconsciously and we totally bombed it? Much more likely, also known as...

The ego

Ah-ha, here's the culprit! The Ego in psychology is the part of the mind that mediates between the conscious and the unconscious. And is responsible for reality testing and a sense of personal identity.

Essentially, The Ego is designed to keep us safe, it also stops us from taking risks and keeps us from harm. Reminding us to keep away from hot things and checking for traffic before crossing the road.

Unfortunately, even though it's meant to keep us safe, it can also block us from achieving our goals, dreams, desires, and growth.

Gurus like Albert Einstein, Jillian Michaels, and Brené Brown have said for years, "Manage your Ego", "The Ego is a hustler", and "Big Egos are big shields for lots of empty space".

And they're not wrong. I know you've heard this before; I have countless times, and this isn't a new breakthrough.

But I don't think that we truly comprehend the limitations we create for ourselves by staying safe. In fact, most people won't even contemplate this in their lifetime.

The only time we do contemplate this, unfortunately, is when we're forced to. The pain of a situation must get so high that it becomes simply unbearable before we decide to act.

In short, if we don't receive the kick up the bum from the universal boot, then nothing will change. And we will still choose safety, thanks to The Ego.

My universal bum-kick

Eight months ago, I was living in Melbourne, Australia, as I have done all my life, with my husband, 4-year daughter, our pussycat and occasionally my adult stepsons.

One night we received a call to say that my elderly father-in-law had had a fall and needed to go into a nursing home as there was no one to look after him. Being 91 and possibly not long for this world, he would need someone to care for and live with him permanently.

My husband and I always knew this day would come, even though we tried to pretend it wouldn't (The Ego). As my husband is British, his dad, lived in... that's right, England.

After many conversations with family members, it became clear that we would be off to England, UK. But there was so much to do!

AN EMPOWERED Life

We needed to say farewell to family and friends, pack all our possessions, empty the house, put everything into storage and prepare our house for rent. Easy, right?

All I can say is Holy Crap, did we have our work cut out for us!

But it got worse...

Because my Father-in-law's health had deteriorated further my husband needed to get on a plane in two weeks and I would follow on a month later with our daughter, after having finished the house.

Shit!

I felt sick in my stomach, how could I possibly do this in a month, on my own? With a 4-year-old? OMG! (The Ego)

After dealing with the initial shock of it all, lots and lots of pity parties and tears later – my mission became clear.

The objective was to get rid of as much stuff as we could, that we didn't intend to keep and pack the rest. I was focused, decisive, completely in flow and took action (The Anointed Sword of Empowerment).

We organised a garage sale for the next weekend.

You know the one that you've been waiting to have for fourteen years but you kept putting it off? Yep, that's the one – organised in a week!

My husband flew out the day after and I kept all the things in the garage and did another garage sale the weekend after.

Without realising, I even inspired some of my neighbours to join me and another six households in our street had garage sales on the same day, drawing a bigger crowd. We all worked together, massively decluttered our homes post Covid-19 and sold a packet of stuff! (The Process)

Then it was time to pack, and I knew I couldn't do this alone, so I called reinforcements and began pulling my resources.

Family, friends, and neighbours were coming over to help move furniture, empty fridges/freezers and take food, pack our belongings into boxes, drop-offs at charity shops, etc.

If you've ever moved house, you can begin to understand this. But if you've ever moved country and not known how long it'll be before you return – you get this.

Throughout this process, and with desperate realisations that my time was quickly running out. I was constantly overwhelmed, having pity parties, and in tears, while trying to stop myself from collapsing – I was exhausted!

I couldn't sleep, I couldn't eat, and I just felt nauseous the whole time.

Make it stop! My head would shout (The Ego).

You can do this! (The Sword of Empowerment)

Just keep going, one more box! (The Process)

I can't do this! (The Ego)

Yes, you can Kleo, you've been in tougher situations than this and you've always smashed it! (The Sword of Empowerment)

Come on, just keep going, one foot in front of the other, you've got this! (The Process)

AN EMPOWERED Life

I kept going and kept going and before I knew it, everything was done.

All finished!

It was Saturday and my sister was driving me to my girlfriend's house with my daughter fast asleep in the back.

It was over. There was nothing else to do, except stop and breathe. I could breathe. And cried lots – tears of relief!

That night I think I had the best night's sleep that I'd ever had in my life.

The next morning my girlfriend made us pancakes, my daughter's favourite, and I can tell you, they were the best darn pancakes I've ever eaten, bar none!

And the next day Miss 4-year-old and I jumped on a plane and flew to Manchester airport to be greeted by my hubby and her daddy, whom we hadn't seen in a month. And cried some more – tears of joy!

The true meaning

Would you call this empowerment?

I never knew the true strength I had until I was pushed to my limit.

To be completely honest, I didn't feel empowered through any of this ordeal. I did feel weak, helpless, tired, anxious, erratic, stressed, and useless a lot though – but never empowered.

Other times I felt focused, driven, in-flow, decisive, accurate, intuitive, efficient, and smashing it – but still not empowered.

But as I've demonstrated throughout this ordeal, The Ego, The Sword of Empowerment and The Process, were all present.

Surprisingly, all three elements were there, and even though they all seemed to fight against each other, they worked in harmony together. Taking it in turns as my thoughts would shift from one to the other to the other.

Weird.

Wait a minute, I've just remembered something.

Arriving at the airport, going through customs and on the plane, people were looking at me funny the whole time. At one stage I remember getting out of my seat and going to the toilet to check my face, as Miss 4-year-old tended to draw lines on my face with her permanent markers.

And there it was...

The biggest, brightest smile on my face and I couldn't stop smiling!

I must admit it did look a bit stalker-y and I could understand why people were looking at me funny. Mate, I would look at me funny if I saw that crazy huge-ass smile.

It was beautiful.

Well, is that Empowerment?

Yes, I do believe it is.

Oh, so it happens after the challenge?

Yes.

And at the start, and in the middle, and the end, and even after that.

AN EMPOWERED *Life*

And every single time you reflect on any challenge you've ever had in your life that you've smashed through – it'll be there too.

It's not something that we have to be given or ordained with like a sword. But you can choose to forge it at your will.

It's not something that we must work hard for like a process. But you can take action and it will be your teammate.

Nor is it controlled or managed by our Ego. But you can make your Ego surrender to it.

So, what does this mean?

Brian Tracey puts it beautifully, "You have within you right now, everything you need to deal with whatever the world can throw at you".

Well, would you look at that?

So, to answer the question: how do you feel empowered?

I suppose it depends on how you choose to define it.

My definition is: Empowerment is already within us and always has been. It has no bounds or limitations, other than what we choose to give it.

What's yours?

Kleo xxx

CHAPTER 6

Vallye Adams

Helping the helpers

Jason, Christian, Vallye Catelynn and Makayla: You are my entire world, the sun, the moon and stars. The air I breathe is for you. Until the end of time, I will love you with every ounce of my soul. Thank you for empowering me and for being my purpose.

" I can promise you, when you find the sweet spot of empowering yourself resulting in the empowerment of others, that realization and feeling of living a truly empowered life... is SO WORTH IT! "
~ Vallye Adams

An empowered life...what does that mean?

Empower: to give someone the "power" to do something. To make someone stronger and more confident, especially in controlling their life and claiming their rights.

So, let's think about this... after thinking about the definition above, here's some questions for you: How do *you* empower yourself? Have you ever really thought about this? How and when do *you* give yourself *power* to do the things? The things you want, things *you* need, things to help *you* reach your goals. That's right, this might come as a shocker, but, I am asking you to answer this question about you. How and when do you empower *yourself* to be stronger, build *your* confidence and own your own life?

These are important and crucial questions that perhaps we don't always ask ourselves. Why are they so important? Because YOU are someone too! You are someone who cannot and should not only empower others but, in my opinion, also focus and work on empowering yourself. Why? If you have ever thought about or actually empowering others and leading an empowered life, I would like to share with you, it is not just about you giving others power to do something. Empowerment is not just helping others to be stronger, more confident and gaining control in their life. I believe before we can truly empower others, before we can encourage and give others power to "do something", and even before we can help make someone else stronger, we must empower ourselves first! Why? When we do, we can and will better empower others.

Maybe this sounds a little selfish. Making it all about ourselves first? Let me explain. By the definition of "empower",

AN EMPOWERED *Life*

the action taken should be to others, correct? In my opinion, an empowered life is living a life where you are empowering yourself to live and own your life to the fullest resulting in you helping empower others to live their best life. That's a mouthful. Maybe read it again. To live a truly empowered life, *you* deserve, everyone deserves, to empower ourselves, as well as empower others.

Wow...that sounds like a lot of 'power'!! Here's my thought: if we can make this happen; give and empower our own life, then wouldn't it make sense we would automatically be able to give and empower others too?? Sounds cut and dry... sounds easy. It's not.

At least not in my world. Certainly, I do not want to give you the notion that I have always believed in and lived fully by this philosophy? NO, absolutely not! *Honest and vulnerable moment*: I struggle every day to focus on and give myself power to do something, to empower myself. I would personally rather empower, help, encourage, do for others first and then, maybe, if there is any extra time, perhaps, work on me. So, what would happen if this thinking was reversed?

My goal here is to "flip the switch", reverse the thinking!! How? By making a conscious steadfast effort every day to find and build my own inner confidence. I have decided it must be a choice and a focus, a set priority, every day. Goal: to channel my own "strength superpowers" *(more information below)* to help empower myself. Why? I have found that when I empower myself, I can and DO empower others in so many ways... and then the best thing is.... the ultimate result is... they empower others too! Empowerment spreads like wildfire!

Make sense?

Here's a little background. This philosophy of mine, on why we *must* empower ourselves so we can better and best empower others, lies in the basis of us knowing and utilizing our own strengths. I believe strongly and have learned everyone has intrinsic, very specific internal "strengths". If we know what our strengths are, understand and leverage them, they can and will be our very own *"Super Powers."* I can personally attest to this!! Many people have always wished to have their own "Super Power" right? Well, we all do and here's the kicker, we've always had them!!

I am so proud to have written a book chapter entitled, *"Strengths are your Superpower"*. This book chapter was featured in a co-authored, International Best-Selling Book, entitled, *"Yes I Can" 16 Success Secrets from Inspiring Women around the World"*. In my chapter, I share my journey of childhood into adulthood. I disclosed how from the ashes of the darkest place of depression and despair, basically, not wanting to go on living, I was able to rise to the brightest cloud in the highest peak of happiness and personal success. I share about my large family, upbringing, and life's passions. Most importantly, I divulged how my initial beliefs and struggles to achieve others' expectations of me versus the result of ultimately achieving my full potential and own desired success was realized.

How? When I learned about and activated my strengths (learned from the *Clifton Strengths Assessment* by Gallup), these became and are truly my "Super Powers".... (insert fireworks here... bammmm!). In this chapter, I showcase ideas on how and where to find your own internal strengths, how to create and use your own "Strength Superpower Sentence (SSPS)" and how and why to build your "Superpower Strength Team". Feel free to read this chapter along with 15 other amazing success stories that will truly inspire your success at, https://www.lulu.com/

shop/vallye-adams/yes-i-can/paperback/product-7jg86r.html?page=1&pageSize=4

Empowering the sweet spot

EmPower YOU + EmPower Others = EmPowered LIFE

Perhaps, if this philosophy was explained in a mathematical formula, it might look like above. Honest fact: I've never been (and never will be) a math person, really, it is not one of my strengths at ALL. Perhaps, visually, this might help?

As I'm sure you've heard and even said this yourself, "easier said than done", right? True. Flipping the switch and practicing this formula, although I say it and believe it, trust me, I still work every single day to achieve it. If you are willing to give this philosophy (or formula) a try, you may just find you can live a truly inspired and empowered life. Is it easy? Nope... but I can promise you, when you find the sweet spot of empowering yourself resulting in the empowerment of others, that realization and feeling of living a truly empowered life... is SO WORTH IT!

Strengths are key. Once you know and learn them, how to leverage them as a power to your own empowerment, the first formula changes a little. When/if you add your strengths, perhaps the formula might look like this:

Strengths/EmPowerYou + EmPowerOthers = EmPowered LIFE

(again, apologies as I have zero math strengths at ALL, so.... just taking a shot!)

When we know our strengths; we can best *divide* and prioritize them into our life. When we do this, they can help create our best self and reach towards our goals. How you divide and apply your strengths into your everyday routine is up to you. However, when you do so, these become the superpowers I mentioned. When you use your strengths to help empower your best self (EmPowering YOU) your empowerment, confidence, will shed, exude, to others. This will help you to empower others to achieve their own success, confidence, best life, (EmPowering Others). Putting these together will enable YOU to feel and lead a very fulfilled and Empowered Life!

Let me share more. Knowing my own intrinsic strengths, i.e. superpowers, has helped me focus on developing my best self and share with others what I am best at. Let me first share with you my own personal CliftonStrength Superpowers.

1. WOO (Winning Others Over)
2. Communication
3. Positivity
4. Includer
5. Activator

I think they explain their meaning, however, if you would like to learn more about these and learn your own strengths, check out the Clifton Strengths Assessment by Gallup. www.gallup.com/cliftonstrengths (*not associated or affiliated with)

When I work and focus on applying, enhancing, and utilizing my strengths (vs weaknesses, things I need to improve upon), I have more control and power over my life. When I use this self-empowerment, I am better equipped to share my best self, share my strengths, talents, and life to empower others. This IS the sweet spot. Once our strength superpowers are mobilized and shared, we are empowered. Once we use our empowerment to empower others we truly live an EmPowered Life… the "sweet spot". This is when we have empowered ourselves to empower others.

Full circle of empowerment

When you put everything together: #1. Knowing and utilizing your strengths. #2. Focus on empowering yourself #3. Results in empowering others, and #4. Living a truly empowered life, chances are, your life's purpose will be clear (or maybe it is already) and comes shining through. So, once we have found and added our "purpose", what does that do to this awesome mathematical formula??

Strengths/EmPowerYou + EmPowerOthers + PURPOSE = EmPowered LIVES (plural, many)

By adding 'purpose' to the mix, now living your empowered life, turns into helping empower multiple lives!! Have you found your purpose?

My purpose. It's what I found when I learned how to use these "superpowers". Again, not only to help others, but to help me help others. Why? Because if you think about the strengths I have (listed above), they confirmed something key. I am a people person. a lover of people. I have always loved and wanted to meet and be around people. My happiness comes from trying to help everyone, *including* everyone, make others happy. My inner joy comes from *communicating* and encouraging others, to see the best and most *positive attributes* in themselves. I love to help others *activate*, take action to reach their highest potential. I strive to *win others over* in the belief they are better than what they believe. I thrive to help make everything, life, better for others.

So knowing all of this, any idea, guess what might be my true passion and purpose? Well, happy to share with you what gets me out of bed every day, really keeps me going, day after 16-hour day, is: first, the absolute love of my family, husband and 3 children.... then, helping to make the world a better place. I know, SO cliché, right?

Nonprofits. *Helping the helpers.* That's my purpose. That is why I am here on this earth, to help the helpers help the world. So sappy and mushy!! I know. But, after many years of self-searching, after many years lacking the ability to *power my own empowerment*, I finally found my SELF and my purpose. I empowered my Super Powers to help empower others to find their own powers and empower others (many, plural). It's what I'll call a full circle, a trifecta of empowerment... making the world a better place... creating truly Empowered Lives!!

Finding the power to persevere

Again, yes, all of this is easier said than done. It's not like you just find your strengths in a fortune cookie, instantly understand what they mean and then poof!! Your fairy godmother appears, waves her magic wand, and presents you with a purpose-filled pumpkin and off you ride off into the sunset of your happily ever after empowered life. Nope. That sounds nice though, right? However, from what I have experienced after almost a half century of living: Life is not a fairy tale. However, if you are willing to work at it, focus on and believe in YOU, I believe you and everyone has the power to be a Superhero!!

So, say you are onboard and willing to give this formula a try. Maybe you already work at making sure to empower yourself, empower others and shine your life's purpose. Either way, chances are you are aware, achieving your ultimate visions of success and life's goals is an ongoing process, a constant work in progress. There are always roadblocks and challenges along the way.

Yes, I have had plenty of them! So, when and how did I decide to implement this formula, and actually apply it?? Well, when I was finally ready to truly and honestly empower myself, to help the helpers and take on this role to make the world a better place, the world decided to shut down, literally.

March 1, 2020. *Etavele* Solutions was born, well, officially opened. It had been born and growing in my mind for decades. This was the day I set sail on the dream of my lifetime, broke free from the shackles of corporate life, and became my own boss. Entrepreneurship, I am your captain!! With $1,000 in the bank, a simple business plan (clearly with little to no math inspiration), many years of experience in the nonprofit sector along with my superpowers and a heartfelt desire to help the helpers, I JUMPED!!!

**Etavele is the word "Elevate", spelled backwards. "Elevate" the nonprofit, the helpers, is the mantra. Like my name, Vallye, I wanted my company name to be different and have a unique and special meaning.

(13 days later…..)

March 13, 2020. The world shuts down, closes, stops. Everyone, everywhere is on lockdown due to Covid-19 Pandemic.

Well, what now? This was definitely not in the business plan. I'm sure you remember, life as we knew it stopped. For me, this was not just a speed bump in the road. This was more like a road just ending. I was driving on a long road in the middle of the desert. Imagine sand and tumbleweed blowing past you. Then suddenly, I am driving with fish and seaweed passing by, at the bottom of the ocean... ahhh a shark!! I know, I know. No one drives at the bottom of the ocean; no roads go or stop in the ocean. Well, no one in my lifetime had ever experienced a global pandemic and shutdown. The timing was unbelievable.

Tell me, who in their sane mind, has any financial sense, knowledge of principles of economics and business, a family, three children, the 2nd starting college a few months later, would decide it was a great time to start their own business, 13 days before a global pandemic?? ME. Granted, I didn't know the fate of the world as I tendered my resignation at my six figure, executive national nonprofit management job and said farewell on February 28th 2020.

Not even the strongest superpowers could fix or change this one. Or could they? Well, I was about to find out. It was now or never, sink or swim, fly high or crash and burn. I was about to put my strengths and this formula to the ultimate test! There was not a book, class, first hand experience, podcast, article, mentor, lecture, meeting, or prayer that could have prepared me, or anyone else for that matter, to open a business at the start of a global pandemic, a complete shutdown.

Where did I start? How did I empower myself? How did I plan to fulfill my dream and sail my "ship" to help the helpers, empower others to make the world a better place? Here's how I put on that cape and kept going when everything and everyone else stopped.

I activated. I communicated. Outreached to and included everyone. Won others over through positivity and perseverance. Sound familiar? I activated my strengths. Call it fight or flight. Call it crazy. Instead of putting on the sweatpants, binge watching the latest Netflix shows, taking some time off, sitting back and waiting on the lockdown to end, I took action and decided to empower myself. Making this decision and actually working on building my confidence, not giving up and staying the course... and keep showing up wasn't easy. The definition of "activate" is *"to make something active or operative"*. I decided now was not the time to remain still, silent, or wait. Now was GO time! This was MY empowerment moment.

How did I activate? Every day, I got up early, dressed in professional attire, styled my hair and make-up, gave myself a pep talk, put a smile on my face and went...walked into the "office". My home office. The office I had been dreaming of for so long. I made a choice. I was not going to let the world stopping, stop me!

Yes, the kids were home, the husband was home, offices, stores, and restaurants, closed. Activating and making the decision to go was only the first step. What could I do to share and *elevate* nonprofit organizations when they were shut down too? Very quickly we all learned we could still *communicate*. We had social media, virtual platforms, Zoom, TEAMS, reels, chat and messaging rooms and more. So, I went to work. Etavele was operational. I thanked the stars above for the WIFI connectivity and began communicating. Some ways:

- Sent emails to nonprofits, some I knew and had worked with, others pure cold outreach.

- Texted family, friends and those I knew in the nonprofit sector and said, lets chat!

- Joined and became active in nonprofit, entrepreneurship, and fundraising Facebook groups, sending messages to as many people as I could.

- Answered and commented on many social media posts, specifically in the nonprofit world, offering ideas and suggestions where I had experience.

- Happily, offered to set up "positive" and forward-thinking virtual calls/meetings, including everyone in the nonprofit industry. At one point, I found myself hosting zoom meetings with up to 30 people from different nonprofit organizations, three times a day.

When all we had was "virtual", virtual networking groups were fantastic. They gave me the opportunity to introduce myself and *Etavele*, share my experience, knowledge, offer ideas and suggestions. On the group meetings, I asked others to share what they were doing to "pivot" (soon, the word of the year). I was proud and excited to share my passion and experience AND I truly learned so much from others as well. After relationships developed during the virtual meetings and because some of the organizations asked, I decided to offer one-hour individual "exploration" calls. These calls/meetings gave me additional time with people/organizations who, of course were not yet clients. This helped developed trust, share more, and enable collaboration; eventually allowing us to make lemonade out of lemons. Looking back, one of the things I am most proud of, is not charging for my time (again, not in the business plan). This was a very difficult time for everyone and allowing the focus to be on the people not the profit, really gave me the opportunity to win others over on me and Etavele Solutions. Again, not the easiest thing to do but it was the best thing to do. Everyone agreed what was true, now, more than ever, even the helpers needed help. And I was ready to help!

Everyone was in the same boat... I called it "pandemic pandemonium". Although we may have been sailing in different sized ships and in different seas, we were all in a storm. When sailing through life, I believe that there are a few 'ships' we all need to succeed. In life and in business: Relationships such as friendships, partnerships, mentorships, kinships are essential. In the nonprofit world, if you know... it's sponsorships!

For me, activating, communicating, creating positive forums including as many people as I could, and winning others over to demonstrate how I could share my strengths and expertise with their organization, became my superpower. That empowerment time and "sweet spot" moment for me allowed me to fully understand and witness firsthand that empowering myself really did lead to the empowerment of others and ultimately the empowerment of many. At a time when so many stopped, I kept going and would not let giving up be an option. Were there setbacks? Absolutely? Were there failures? 100% and always will be; however, not letting the failures, mistakes and setbacks stop me or my belief was and is the key. I believed in and still believe in the formula.

Strengths/EmPowerYou + EmPowerOthers + PURPOSE= EmPowered LIVES (plural, many)

I believe the reason Etavele Solutions didn't sink with the pandemic is because after two and a half years of staying the course, I never gave up and always showed up. I continue to use, divide and prioritize my strengths to empower myself. I make it a priority everyday, build relationships, stay connected and lean on and learn from mentors, family and friends. Empowering others, sharing my purpose and passion to help the helpers, cultivating all of the "SHIPS". This formula, equation or for my math delinquent self, a philosophy, is leading to many empowered lives AND the continued journey and sailing of Etavele Solutions setting sail!

Vallye Adams

One of the most globally devastating times in this century has become for me, one of my most rewarding, successful and best times. The power of empowerment. The word 'power' is spelled right in the word. Ladies and gentlemen, we all have it. Use it. Share it. Live it.

While writing this chapter, my family and I experienced the tragic, unimaginable and unexpected loss of my 13-year-old niece, Lilly. She was riding her bike home from school and was struck by a hit and run driver. The loss and despair for our entire family is immense. It is at our darkest times, saddest hour, we try to remember the philosophy to never give up, to live for those who could not and remember and cherish the beautiful memories, dreams and life of those we have lost.

Using my purpose and passion to continue to *help the helpers*, which was also a characteristic of and a huge part of Lilly's personality, I would like those who read this chapter to share, EMPOWER me and be a part of sharing, EMPOWERING others, in Lilly's memory.

I will create a page on Etavele Solutions website (www.etavelesolutions.com) entitled "LOVE FROM LILLY". Please visit and share your empowerment stories, love and memories of lost ones, and your own stories of life, loss, challenges, successes, and triumph. Please share with me your favorite nonprofit or charity organization and why it is so important to you. Every month for the next year, I will select a nonprofit and donate to a nonprofit organization in Lilly's memory. It will be shared on the site. Thank you for your love and empowerment.

With Love and Empowerment, Vallye Adams,

Vallye Adams

AN EMPOWERED *Life*

Dedication:

> Lilly,
> I will say not good bye,
> but send you off with endless love
> As you spread your beautiful wings and fly
>
> Go play and rest with the angels in heaven above.
> Although you will be out of our sight after today,
> We know you will always be with us, at our side, in every way.
> You will be the brightest sun rays on our face when we play in the pool...
> We will hear your laughter and see your smile in your brothers, Makayla and all of your friends from school
>
> Lilly, We will not say goodbye
> Instead, look up into the sky.
> We'll say hello, and watch you continue to shine and sparkle in the stars...
> As the family love we share, will forever stay in your heart and in ours.
>
> Let's not say goodbye
> but, please say hello to all of our family in heaven above
> as I know they will greet you with the biggest hugs and so much love...
> And then you all will celebrate, not a goodbye,
> but instead have the best "Lilly's here" party up in the sky!!
>
> I don't want to say goodbye Lilly
> but rather watch for the signs,
> Because you're so very special

Vallye Adams

We all know there could be many kinds...
Butterflies, cardinals, dreams or a cool breeze,
we will wait and be ready, visit us anyway you please,

Today is not goodbye, Lilly
As You'll be at our side, watching over, guiding and protecting us all,
Taking care first and foremost, of your mom, Peter, Marshall and Paul.
We know you'll wrap your arms around us, comfort us, ease our fears and dry our tears,
because even though strong we will try,
there will be many times we will cry

This is not a goodbye because
Our family bond is one that can never be broken
but Lilly, know your memory and our love for you will always be felt, shown and spoken.
Every Meal, every birthday,
every holiday, every day
Every time our family is together,
"hello Lilly, we know you are here, you are with us, always and forever,

I will not say goodbye .
but say LOVE YOU forever and always
even though we are apart.
Aunt Vallye, Uncle Jason, Makayla, Catelynn and Christian love you Lilly. Forever in our hearts.

Kylie James
Coach, Mentor, People Strategist, Author and Speaker, Australia.

CHAPTER 7

Kylie James

Standing at a crossroads

To seven year old Kylie, I'm so glad I found you again - you are magic!

And to my partner Sean, thank you for being there through the tough moments, for loving me when I didn't love myself and for being my champion.

"Listen to what your heart and soul is telling you - don't overthink it"
~ Kylie James

Taking the leap

I was your typical corporate warrior. I went to university, got a good job, got promoted, and lived comfortably. From the outside, life was heading in the right direction. From the inside, my self-worth and esteem was low. By the time I had turned 40, my inner spark had disappeared.

In February 2022, I made a huge leap. That leap represented freedom, taking my power back, backing myself and believing in myself.

I left a safe, permanent career that paid extremely well to take my business from being a side hustle to a full-time gig. I became an entrepreneur and began chasing my dreams! I invested in myself, asked for help and dug deep to find my spark again.

Was I scared? Yes.

Was I excited? Yes.

Was I ready for a new adventure? Heck yes!

Little did I know what would lie ahead. There were tears, anger, frustration, happiness, laughter and joy. When I look back, I describe it as mayhem! Now my life is magic!

What if???

When I was growing up, I never really felt like I belonged anywhere. Not with my family, at school, university or at work. I tried to fit-in however, it didn't seem to matter what I did, I just couldn't find my tribe.

AN EMPOWERED *Life*

I grew up in a hard working family. My parents gave my brother and I every opportunity to succeed in whatever we wanted to do in life. I got my first career break when I won a graduate role. I moved 4000 kilometres from Cairns to settle in Canberra and start what would be a successful 20 year career. I grew my experience and skill set and climbed the ladder.

There were some twists and turns within these years. My confidence levels and self-doubt would go up and down. It wasn't until I invested in my own personal development and I rediscovered who I was as a person that I found where I belong in life.

People had always naturally seen me as a person whom they could turn to for advice. I was known as someone who would listen and help solve problems without any judgment.

In February 2021, I started my coaching business as a side hustle. My goal was to empower others to create a magical life. I felt inspired each time I walked out of a coaching session with a client.

The business started slowly, and built over time. The more I coached people, the more I was inspired. I had the honour of watching clients achieve some amazing results. Not only had they found their mojo again, so had I!

By September 2021 I was thinking, 'Hang on a sec, I might be onto something here'. I kept dreaming about what my future could look like. I kept asking myself "what if?"

What if, I could make this side hustle into a full-time business?

What if, I could make this business the next chapter of my career and also let it become the best chapter so far?

Kylie James

Life happens for us, not to us

On Thursday, 10 February 2022, I woke up and for the first time in my adult life I didn't have a job to go to. I didn't have a boss. I was my own boss running my own business!

I had planned how I would spend my first day as I knew I needed a self-care day. I hadn't really processed the enormity of what I had just done. I had given two months notice at work so the countdown to my last day was quite long. Work was busy so there hadn't been much time to pause and take a breath.

That night I went out to dinner to celebrate the first day of the next chapter of my life. Friday came along and I spent most of it preparing for a facilitation day the following week for a client.

On the Saturday, it was all different. I fell in a heap. I felt like the world was crashing in around me. The emotions were raw and real. I sat on the couch by myself and cried for hours. Everything had hit me at once. It was overwhelming.

The question that kept rolling around in my mind was "What had I done?".

I had been in my permanent career in corporate for 20 years. I had achieved a lot, worked on some great projects, met some amazing people who had turned into friends and climbed the ladder to a leadership position. Overall, it was a very successful career.

The last few years had taken a toll though. The inspiration and motivation to keep climbing the ladder was gone. I was burnt out, tired, lonely and struggling to find my purpose. I was working long hours each night and on weekends.

AN EMPOWERED *Life*

As much as I tried to get out of the cycle of putting work before everything else in my life, I kept falling back into the trap of letting it completely consume me. My whole identity was wrapped up in my job and career. I didn't know who I was outside of work. I had lost myself.

One day I woke up and I said to myself, "If this was the last day of my life, how would people describe me?". The answer was "Kylie was a great worker. She worked hard at her career".

Boom! That was my life changing moment! That was when I decided things needed to change. I had so many other dreams that I wanted to achieve and it was time to go chase them!

Let's rewind the clock a bit...

Here are two photos of me. No make-up, no filter, no photoshopping in either photo. Raw and real.

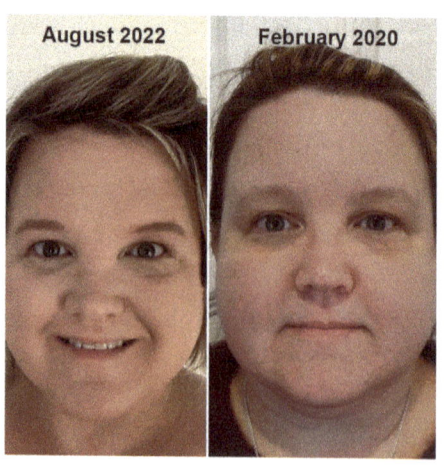

2019 and 2020 were big years. I went through lots of "stuff" - mainly work related. It was difficult to not take home how I was feeling though. Most mornings, I was in tears before I left the house. I had to pull myself together on the half-hour drive across town and put on a smile that was really a facade. I was pretty broken emotionally, physically and mentally. I was burnt out, overwhelmed, sad, lonely, tired and had little energy. Some may say I was even depressed. Weight kept piling on. Clothes didn't fit. I had constant stomach pains from my anxiety. I was a shell of the person who I was born to be. Yet, I was still trying so hard to find her!

Fast forward to August 2022. You might notice some physical differences between the photos. For me, I notice the changes that you can't see. What I notice is:

- the increase in confidence, self worth and self belief
- a person who is living life aligned with their values
- a person who has found a place where she finally belongs without feeling like she has to fit-in and be the same as everyone else
- a person who no longer has stomach pains and her anxiety is almost gone.

Best of all, I notice a person wakes up each day looking forward to what she is doing, is much more present with people in her life and feels alive again! And yet, my transformation is not yet done! The better I feel the more I want to do!

The path to freedom

It wasn't one big thing. It was lots of things. It was saying YES to investing time, money and energy into myself!

When I was at my lowest point, I thought it was going to be all about losing weight and getting fitter as that was always my story. Instead, it has ended up being all about finding the fun in life again.

Sitting down and assessing my life and where it was at, helped me make shifts in my mindset, gave me confidence and most of all, took the overwhelm out of feeling like everything had to be different. It highlighted the big things to focus on and gave me permission to let the other stuff just be. It showed me where I was doing well and also where I could improve. It showed me that if I made one small tweak, there was a ripple effect to other parts of my life.

By showing me a different way of looking at myself and my life, I was able to take my power back and change my story.

Embracing who I was, backing myself and acknowledging that it is okay to be different to others has meant freedom. It's allowed me to achieve a level of inner peace that I had been searching for.

So what did I actually do?

- I reconnected with my coach who challenged me to think differently.
- I re-assessed my Values so I could make decisions that were aligned with them.
- I started my coaching business as a side hustle.
- I left a 20 year career that no longer inspired me.
- I decluttered my house, social media and wardrobe.
- I made decisions about the people who I was surrounding myself with.
- I started forgiving myself for all the not-so-proud moments I have had over the past 40 years that I had previously been mentally beating myself up about. I am not a rule-breaker so even small things I did, I saw them as major mistakes. To other people, it would have been experiencing life and growing up!
- I started liking my body and appreciating all the amazing things it has done even though it isn't perfect (e.g. thank

you legs for helping me walk four days of the Machu Picchu trail!)
- I started liking myself again! This was a big piece of the puzzle!
- I started saying goodbye to people pleasing and perfectionism.
- I started stopping myself from comparing myself and my life to everyone else! Comparisonitis is real....

None of these things are easy to navigate, yet if you take on the challenge, it is so rewarding!

I found myself again. I found freedom. I started to smile again. I started to dance around the house to music like 7 year old Kylie used to!

The process was hard and at times messy. It didn't happen overnight. There was mayhem. There were tears. I was tested and tested again. Yet, there was also lots of laughter and so much magic!

My partner Sean, was definitely on the rollercoaster of emotions with me over this entire time. The best part of the magic is that he is still here - waking up next to me each day and saying "Hello, beautiful little Kylie", cheering me on as I have entered this new chapter of my life where I am thriving rather than surviving.

Becoming visible in my own world

When I decided I wanted more than simply working hard for the rest of my life, I knew I was ready for my breakthrough moment. I knew I wanted to change the world. I knew what I wanted to do. The big piece of the puzzle that was missing was that I needed to show up differently in my own world. I needed to step out of the shadows, back myself and become visible.

Shortly after I opened my business, I paid to participate in a business coaching group. Given I had always been employed by someone else, I really had no idea how to run all the backend processes of a business.

The lead of the group wanted us to start promoting ourselves and our businesses on social media. The thought of doing this made me feel sick! I had to take my invisibility cloak off!

This task was a big deal for me. It represented a change in identity for me. It meant I had to change how I saw myself as a coach and what I could offer clients.

The reality was - if I didn't make myself more visible, how would I get any clients? How could my business be successful if I stayed hidden? If I didn't show-up, I wasn't being a role model for my clients as I wasn't walking the talk.

What I absolutely loved about being part of this coaching group was that it gave me confidence to change. I started posting about my story and my business. My group gave me feedback, cheered me on and supported me along the way.

Fast forward 18 months, I resigned from my corporate job and am now helping others become visible in their own world!

No matter what role you have in life, showing up with confidence and as our true self looks and feels different for everyone. Some people can do it with ease and others struggle to walk out the door each day.

By taking the steps to become more visible, it has shown me that not only do I have the strength inside of me, I can also put my hand on my heart and say that I am walking the talk that many of my clients are looking at me for inspiration.

In return, what I have loved is that all of my clients commit to taking action, no matter how small, shifting them one step closer to becoming confident in shining their bright light and becoming visible in their own world.

What's next?

In 2020, I was a corporate warrior working long hours and hiding in the shadows. Today, I am thriving in life running my coaching business and being authentically me.

My vision is to empower others to live their life on their own terms particularly as they transition from one chapter to the next in life. Transitioning between different chapters of life takes commitment, perseverance, patience and vulnerability. Whether you are ready for a career or job change or you want to turn your whole life upside down, staying stuck doing the same thing won't get you anywhere.

You don't need to fit-in all the time. Have the courage to be your true self and chase your dreams.

There is no quick fix or magic wand. Changing your life involves digging deep, being curious and asking the tough questions so you can design a new future. Change is the one constant in today's society - it won't always be smooth sailing. If you stick with it though, you will reap the benefits.

AN EMPOWERED *Life*

What are my next steps?

My dreams are abundant. I have started a community on Facebook for women in their mid-lives to help them navigate all the lifestyle challenges without feeling embarrassed, guilty or apologetic. You can also check out my website for more information on my other programs, Inspiring Change and Nine to Thrive Corporate Coaching.

For me, this is just the beginning.

When I reflect back, I feel a bit like Cinderella. I made a wish and it has come true. I still pinch myself everyday that I am doing something I absolutely love with incredible people.

I am now living the best years of my life which is why I love helping others rediscover their spark so they can make their life magical.

I believe that everyone has a beautiful life story. I hope by reading mine, it inspires you to take a look at yours and realise that amongst everything, there is so much gold and so much magic. Sometimes, we just have to dig a little deeper to find it.

My number one piece of advice? Reach out to a coach and talk to them about how they can support you to get started on the changes that you want to make. It is an absolute privilege for a coach to be on a person's support team. The best part? We get to be your accountability buddy!

"A dream is a wish your heart makes." ~ Cinderella

Until we chat, keep on smiling. :)

Hugs

Kylie xx

CHAPTER 8

Lisa Ohtaras

Change your thoughts change your life

To all the Ascended Masters, The Divine and my Higher Self, I am eternally grateful for your teachings, guidance, unconditional love, support, spiritual gifts, and the work I have the privilege and honour to conduct.

Thank you to all my family, friends, soul sisters, soul brothers, and clients who have assisted me on my spiritual journey to date and continue to assist me. You all know who you are. I am very grateful!

"The breakdown is the prelude to the breakthrough."
~ Lisa Ohtaras

Lisa Ohtaras

My story begins with the warning signs of Multiple Sclerosis over twenty-five years ago.

Although I appeared to have it all in the physical world; I married the man I fell in love with, we had two beautiful children, a wonderful, loving supportive family, the dream home, working in the career of my choice, and then halfway into my married life, my health became seriously compromised.

My SOUL deliberately created multiple health challenges at one time to spiritually awaken me.

A consultation with my family's usual naturopath was not possible as she was on holiday. After seeing a highly recommended naturopath, and being assessed by her, I was informed I had the warning signs of Multiple Sclerosis (M.S.) which is an autoimmune disease. M.S. was then incurable and remains incurable to this day by traditional medicine.

The numbness and pain, alternating with pins and needles in my hands and arms, feet and limbs were troublesome, to say the least. My other symptoms such as insomnia, night sweats, visual disturbances, and chronic fatigue were highly concerning.

One month following my initial visit with the naturopath and strictly adhering to her instructions; resting and taking all the prescribed vitamin supplements and herbal teas, I was reassessed by the naturopath. I was informed my condition had become worse. The news was devastating for me.

The external remedies had no positive benefits for me because my Soul wanted the inner work to be done.

My symptoms had worsened because my Soul wanted me to make the connection to my inner self so I could heal from within.

AN EMPOWERED *Life*

My spiritual awakening was my gift to heal from within...

That same day the Angelic Beings of Light began to communicate with me and urged me to do the inner work, and it started with changing my thoughts and deeper still, changing the beliefs that created the thoughts. I noted subtle yet obvious changes and improvements in my physical body from the onset of the inner work and I began to heal.

Years later, following my own self-healing, I was informed by my Soul, that the health challenges I was experiencing were created by my Soul and were uncreated by my Higher Self after doing the inner work. My Higher Self wanted to see me doing the inner work.

Serious health challenges cannot heal with the same thoughts which created the issues...

A person cannot heal an illness with the same thoughts which created the health challenge. Hence why I did not see any improvement in my symptoms and condition when I attempted to heal solely with external aids, as my thoughts remained very much the same or at times became even more negative.

A major component in reframing my beliefs was a deep forgiveness practice, forgiveness of other people combined with self-forgiveness. This practice alongside daily meditation, which deepened my capacity for insight, was instrumental in restoring my body to wellness which was out of balance and out of alignment. I quickly began to realise I was more than my name, personality, and nationality.

It took me two years to heal from within and restore my health and balance to normal, without taking any medication whatsoever.

Energy practices positively helping people, became of great interest to me. I decided to explore energy healing and I studied the Diploma of Energetic Healing at college and loved the education I received, and enjoyed spending time with the people I interacted with.

Everything I needed to know to heal myself was within me...

My body was the barometer of my Soul. Every person's body is the barometer of their Soul. My Soul wanted me to connect with my inner self, heal from within, expand my Soul's consciousness and my spirit's awareness, and discover my Sacred Contract.

Whilst I was studying at college my twenty-year nursing career ended. I was Divinely guided to commence living the next phase of my life fulfilling my Sacred Contract.

I loved, and continue to love, working my Sacred Contract helping animals with energy healing and people with energetic healing, soul healing, and intuitive coaching. I help a person to have a greater awareness of themselves, their life, and past lives and how to heal different areas through several modalities, including Soulful Forgiveness and Self Forgiveness/Self-Acceptance and Atonement, mediumship, and channelling.

AN EMPOWERED Life

Following my inner healing and having my health restored to normal and being in alignment, I made a distinct observation.

My many core negative beliefs, and limiting beliefs led to sabotaging behaviours that were permeating different areas of my life. I observed core negative beliefs playing out in my everyday living when I was very unwell with the M.S. warning signs and after my inner healing.

Although at first I did major forgiveness and self-forgiveness work during my personal development and inner healing, less attention was given to core negative beliefs, and limiting beliefs which led to continued self-sabotage.

My spiritual awakening led me to living consciously...

Beliefs come from parents, grandparents, family, friends, affiliates, groups, associations, society, and teachings.

Our subconscious mind is composed of beliefs, paradigms, conditioning, suppressed memories, repressed memories, teachings, and thousands of memories from past lives.

Often what is playing out in our reality is due to a belief within our subconscious mind.

All of my thoughts held a particular vibration. And whatever I thought, whether it was from my conscious awareness or my subconscious mind, was part of my reality.

Low vibrational negative beliefs are very much victim archetype energy, which is victim consciousness.

The Law of Attraction is always in motion...

The universe will always support any belief a person has. This happens by the Law of Attraction. Like, attract like.

So, I started to make a note of my core negative beliefs in my life and then asked myself the question. Does this belief positively support and empower me and the life I want to create and live?

If the answer was a definite NO, the belief does not positively support or empower me in any way, shape, or form, then I did the inner work to own the belief, embrace it, then collapse it and replace the belief with a positive, empowering belief. Then I allowed the universe to support me with my new positive, empowering belief.

This is a powerful exercise for all kinds of beliefs, from the crippling beliefs that stop us from positively moving forward, to the ones that inform our smaller everyday decisions and behaviours. Here is an example of changing a belief and transforming the energy from negative to positive and empowering.

Old Belief
In my mind, I transformed the belief that I must do everything in the home, from household chores, cooking, laundry, ironing and more to a positive belief.

New belief
I have support from my husband, children, and other people, to help me with the household chores, cooking, and other ways to make my life easier.

AN EMPOWERED *Life*

That same day I did the inner work, my then-husband cooked dinner and helped with household chores. He then began to cook more frequently than he had previously done. Then my children started helping with kitchen chores, something they had never done before.

The results were positive, empowering, and amazing.

Once I changed my negative belief to a positive belief the universe worked its miracle by the Law of Attraction and supported my new belief.

Mistakes are purposeful and part of the Soul's evolution...

Mistakes will be made throughout our lives. Without mistakes, we cannot grow.

The Soul creates the situations, circumstances, conditions, and events for the purpose of spiritual growth to help the healing of our Soul and to expand the Soul's consciousness.

I continue to observe the language I use toward myself, and I try to be very mindful of how I speak to other people.

When speaking with people, I try as best as possible to convey positive information and wisdom with the intention to help support and empower people.

Change your beliefs and transform your life...

When I catch myself thinking, or worse, speaking a core negative belief, I immediately identify the belief and see whether it belongs to me from this lifetime or if it's a negative belief or limiting belief that belongs to my Soul, my inner beings or elsewhere.

If the negative belief is not mine, I clearly say:

Dear Higher Self,

This core negative belief (state the belief) is not mine. The belief belongs to my Soul or has originated elsewhere, and it does not positively serve me. I acknowledge that it exists within me. I own it and embrace it. I now request to please clear the belief (state the belief), transmute the belief and energy into light and love and return it back to the point of creation where it originated. Thank you, I am very grateful for the experience.

By doing this process I have helped heal an aspect of my Soul, an inner being or multiple inner beings or perhaps other external energy I have absorbed. My Soul always rejoices when I do this work, I feel the joy of my inner beings permeate within me.

If the negative belief is clearly mine that I have created, I say:

Dear Higher Self,

I acknowledge that this negative belief (I state my belief) belongs to me. I own it and I embrace it. The belief no longer serves me. I now request to please transform the belief (I state the belief), transmute the belief into light and love and return it back to the point of creation where it originated. Thank you, I am grateful for this experience.

My belief system was disempowering me for many years until I learned to harness the energy of identifying my core negative beliefs and limiting beliefs. Subsequently, I worked on the beliefs to own and embrace them, then reframe the energy and stories I was telling myself about myself, into positive empowering

AN EMPOWERED *Life*

beliefs and stories. This enabled me to create the reality that I wanted, rather than living my life by default, creating things that I did not want.

This is an art in constant progress, as my Soul is constantly bringing to the surface of my being, past experiences from previous incarnations for me to heal.

The realisation of the importance of positive self-talk is very apparent to me.

A person can create an amazing life when core negative beliefs, limiting beliefs and sabotaging behaviours have been addressed and reframed.

You can find that empowerment in specific situations can happen very quickly when negative beliefs are identified and addressed.

We often tell ourselves unproductive stories relating to our family unit, our youth, the things we did and didn't do, the things we said and didn't say, our failures, disappointments, betrayals, our experiences, and the way other people treated us. We sometimes stay stuck in this energy, which is unproductive, unsupportive, and very disempowering.

Regardless of what the situation is and who it is related to, everything that happens throughout my life and the life of other people is related to spiritual growth.

There is a growth opportunity within all of us when anything happens, whether it be of a positive nature or negative nature. I have learned on my spiritual journey that lessons are constantly forthcoming and there is always an opportunity for growth to be done. Every experience has been created by my Soul in a co-creation process with another person or a group of people, which allows me to heal something or energy within me.

If my experience is unpleasant and I do not like what has transpired or what may be transpiring, I see the opportunity to heal the situation. This incarnation is about growth, and we are here to experience the good, pleasant, very good, excellent, bad, unpleasant, very bad and more.

I live my life with an attitude of gratitude...

Regardless of the situation, whether it be pleasant or unpleasant, I always give gratitude to the universe and my Soul for allowing me to have the experience to help evolve my Soul and my spirit.

When I have a pleasant experience, I am always so grateful for whatever has transpired. I thank God, my Soul and my Source for my experiences. I feel humbled to have had the experience and the goodness which has transpired.

Whenever something unpleasant, bad or negative happens, of course, I do not like it. However, I will look at the situation and see the growth opportunity and the lesson I am being presented with. When I do not learn the lesson, my Soul will repeat it until I have understood it. It may not be with the same situation, person or people; however, the energy will be similar. It is up to me to learn from my experience. All the answers I seek are within me, they are not with other people.

And since learning that what happens to me is not punishment, it is part of my Soul's evolution, I no longer live the victim archetype and I stopped many years ago living in victim land.

AN EMPOWERED *Life*

Letting go of energy that does not serve me...

Without hesitation I will let go of the energy which has been created, knowing holding onto negative energy is totally unproductive and serves no positive purpose. I always do the appropriate growth whether that be Soulful Forgiveness and Atonement work, Self Forgiveness/Self-Acceptance and Atonement & Energy healing.

I also use Letter Writing to express my emotions (which is for me to personally release my emotions). I do not send or give letters to other people unless they are of a positive, pleasant nature. I use the Emotional Freedom Technique – also known as EFT & Tapping, to clear negative beliefs or limiting beliefs and use powerful beautiful Prayers.

As I have done deeper work on myself and evolved, I have observed the calibre of the energetic healing work I conduct has changed.

My work is much deeper than in the past. As I have evolved so has the depth of the sacred work I conduct. I also channel light language during energetic healing sessions to clear abundance blocks in the emotional, financial, and spiritual domains.

Moving forward...

My future work will incorporate remote energetic healing and Soulful Forgiveness and Atonement, Self Forgiveness/Self-Acceptance and Atonement and Energetic Healing, and Spiritual Intuitive Coaching. I will be focusing my energy, skills and knowledge on helping people who are living with illness, and also people who are aware they are going to transition to the inner dimension, the spirit world, and would like to go over in a peaceful state of being. I work at the Soul level clearing and releasing people from emotional wounds they have acquired during this incarnation and previous lifetimes.

Freeing one's Soul to be able to transition to the inner dimension in peace is one of the greatest gifts a person can give to themselves. The work I conduct is gentle, non-invasive and frees people so they can be at peace when they are in the inner dimension.

It is such a privilege and wonderful honour to be able to facilitate the sacred work I conduct. The transformation of people's lives I have witnessed following the Soulful Forgiveness and Atonement & Self Forgiveness/Self-Acceptance & Atonement & Energetic Healing is truly amazing.

My parting gift...

My spiritual journey and Soul evolution has taught me beneficial wisdom I would like to share:

1. Treat every person you encounter throughout your life the way you wish to be treated, with respect and kindness, or treat the person the way they wish to be treated.
2. Serious health challenges and life-threatening illnesses cannot be transformed and healed with the same thoughts which created the illness.
3. Letting go of negative beliefs and limiting beliefs not only transforms energy, but it also results in a much better quality of life, allowing people to live their passion and dream life.

AN EMPOWERED *Life*

4. Mistakes are part of the Soul's journey. Be kind to yourself when you make a mistake. See the growth opportunity and the lesson you were given. Forgive yourself and other people when you are hurt in any way. Holding onto negative emotions is unproductive and serves no positive purpose, you are hurting yourself.

5. You are on planet Earth to learn, grow, heal from within, change, transform and evolve the Soul and your spirit (the physical entity part of you). Let go of all emotions which do not serve you in a positive manner. Be kind and gentle to yourself.

"Everything you need to know is contained within you."~ Lisa Ohtaras.

Infinite blessings,

Lisa Ohtaras

Aldwyn Altuney

Known as the Media Queen, Aldwyn Altuney is a photojournalist with 38 years' experience in TV, radio, print and online media, Australia.

CHAPTER 9

Aldwyn Altuney

From depressed & suicidal to inspiring truth & good news

"A small group of thoughtful people can change the world. Indeed, it's the only thing that ever has."
~ Margaret Mead

Growing up in Sydney's northern beaches watching hours and hours of mainly negative mainstream news at home, I grew up depressed and angry with the world.

I was bullied from the age of six. Fellow students would pick on me because of my name, the food I took to school and the clothes I wore.

Anything they could pick on, they did. I felt invisible and that I didn't belong here even though I grew up in a loving household.

I have Greek, Turkish and Ukrainian heritage. As all three countries have been at war with each other over the previous century, I call myself the 'love child' now! Having European background, especially from Turkey where my parents grew up, it was the social norm that the men would hang out with the men and women would hang out with the women.

My dad spent more time with my brother than me growing up and, because of that, I felt some rejection from him at an early age.

Soon afterwards, I began clashing with my mum. My parents would say, "Why can't you be like your brother?"

Nick was the studious, well-behaved one in the family. He thought scientifically (like my dad) whereas I was creative (like my mum). Not feeling like I belonged anywhere, I started rebelling from an early age and began running away from home at age 13. Ironically, I was also the number one ranked Australian junior table tennis player at the time! I released my anger through the sport and developed a killer forehand smash.

At age 15, my dad was fed up with my constant rebellion. When I arrived home around 5am the morning after a Halloween party, he kicked me out of the home and said, "You're not my daughter anymore."

I moved into a crazy household in Manly that day, with a drug-addicted drummer, his alcoholic mother and drug-dealing sister. I began working two part-time jobs – earning around $5 per hour to cover my rent of $50 per week. It was a complete party house with non-stop music and jamming until sunrise each morning.

AN EMPOWERED *Life*

After six months of this, with my boyfriend lying to me and cheating on me, there came a turning point. I remember The Pretenders' song 'Don't Get Me Wrong' playing on the turntable and seeing my best friend at the time, kissing and cuddling my boyfriend on our bed. I was 16 at the time and started bawling my eyes out. I called my mum in tears and said, "I can't handle this anymore."

She said, "Come home," which I did. Even though my dad was not happy about it, initially, he gave me another chance and I ended up studying very hard with my brother.

Turning point

I had gone from Dux of North Balgowlah Primary School to failing everything in Year 11 at Mosman High School.

I changed schools at the start of Year 12 to Forest High School, which was another turning point in my life.

I discovered 'the grass is not always greener on the other side' and started to appreciate my parents and family much more.

I qualified to do a Bachelor of Arts in Communication (Media) degree at the University of Canberra (UC) from 1992 to 1994.

While there, the role of Editor of the university newspaper, CUrio, became available. I applied three times before I was offered the position. I took the fortnightly publication from 24 pages to 48 pages and had 30 contributors, which I coordinated. I became the longest serving editor at the paper and loved the power the media had to affect change in the community.

Aldwyn Altuney

The media was a wonderful way to share my voice on what I felt were injustices in the world and help make it a better place to live. I wrote a story about anti-duck shooting, with the headline 'Go and Get Ducked!' and about issues that moved me in some way, including battery farming of chickens, female circumcision, and stories about protecting the environment.

By the time I graduated from university, I received High Distinctions in my majors of TV Production and Photojournalism. This was the start of what ended up being a lucrative career in the media for me. I went on to work as a journalist on TV, in radio and print media across Australia and internationally.

Since then, I have interviewed stars including Charlie Sheen, Jewel, Vanilla Ice, Hugh Jackman, Russell Crowe, Cyndi Lauper, Debbie Harry (Blondie), Alby Mangels, Jimmy Barnes, Jimeoin, and Mikey Robins, among others. I worked as a journalist at The Daily Mercury in Mackay, The Coffs Harbour Advocate, Queensland Times in Ipswich, Satellite Newspapers in Brisbane, Rave and Time Off in Brisbane, the Gold Coast Bulletin and Sun Community Newspapers (where I was a Journalist/Sub Editor for 5 years).

In 2005, I invested $7000 in my first personal development course in the Hunter Valley, NSW. To this day, 17 years later, I have invested more than $500,000 in business and marketing courses, as well as many different modalities of personal development. This has been invaluable for the growth of my business and myself.

I fell pregnant in 2009 and miscarried naturally after nine weeks. I was 36. This was very hard emotionally and I did a few women's workshops after that to help me heal. I have had a few near-death experiences in life, including having a peritonsillar abscess in my throat in 2014, which flared up after emceeing for

AN EMPOWERED *Life*

Colin Hay (lead vocalist of Men at Work who sang the famous song 'Down Under' in 1980) at the Woodford Folk Festival on the Sunshine Coast. This experience made me appreciate my life like never before.

Hundreds of Facebook messages of condolence came through and I began to shed tears of gratitude for all the amazing people in my life.

I wondered: "If I were to die, who would show up at my funeral? What kind of legacy would I leave? What do I want to create for my life?"

Great questions which I often re-visit and reflect on. I've attended women's retreats, weekend workshops and training since then to help me discover my essential power as a woman.

We meditated, did yoga, chanting, dancing, women's sharing circles, inner child healing and artwork, along with moving meditations, shadow, breath, vertical core and conscious connection work.

I have also learned to trust the masculine again through supportive medicine journeys and shamanic rituals honouring the divine feminine and masculine.

I have since realised that I do not need to lead my life in a masculine way and that it is just as important to receive as it is to give – and to trust myself more. The women's work with various mentors has helped me on this journey. The sisterhood circles I have participated in have been amazing for me to help me connect with my best feminine self and appreciate other women for how amazing they are.

Aldwyn Altuney

Blessing in disguise

When I first moved to the Gold Coast in January 2000, I never planned to stay there. My goal was always to live in America, so I rented apartments for the first two years. I was a very busy journalist at the time, so I put an advertisement in the Gold Coast Bulletin for a suitable place.

I received a call from a guy called Lee, who said he had a place for rent in Main Beach across from the ocean. That sounded perfect, so I popped in to see him and the apartment and said I wanted to rent it.

At the time, Lee was a guy in his early 20s (looked like a surfer) and his young 18-year-old girlfriend was pregnant and lying on the bed. I gave him about $1000 in rent and bond and he gave me the keys.

When I went back to the apartment, there was rubbish all over the floor and benchtops, rotten eggs and food in the sink and the door to the balcony would not close.

I suddenly had this sinking feeling in my stomach. Something did not feel right. So I knocked on the door of the apartment next door and asked if they knew if the previous people were going to clean the apartment. They asked if I had spoken to the manager, which I hadn't. When I saw the manager, he angrily said, "Lee owes me 3 weeks in rent!" He was furious and so was I. Lee was not the owner! I gave the manager the keys and cried for about a week.

I could not believe someone would do that or that I fell for such a con artist! After that experience, I decided I wasn't going to rent anymore and bought the house in Southport on the Gold Coast that I still live in to this day 20 years later. So, in hindsight, it was a blessing in disguise.

I believe in karma. What comes around, goes around 10-fold – and not necessarily by the same people who rip others off or do harm! Karma is about cause and effect. What happens to a person, happens because they caused it with their actions. So, if you want great things to happen in your life, do great things for others.

Commitment – at last!

I have a confession to make. It's taken me 7 years and I've finally done it! I have had commitment and intimacy issues with men for YEARS! In fact, since my boyfriend of 4 years strangled and almost killed me one night when I was 22, I've had this attitude that I don't need men for anything, and I'll be just fine on my own!

After years of doing 'part-time' relationships, friends with benefits and lovers, I have finally committed to a man again! And he's not the kind of guy I would have normally committed to, which is perfect, because clearly the kinds of guys I've attracted in the past and how I was in those relationships, have brought me to where I am now. When I became 38, I freaked out because I hadn't had any children yet. I thought when I was growing up that I'd have kids between ages 30 and 35. The clock was ticking fast, so I went on the hunt – online dating like a crazy woman.

"Don't mention BABIES on the first date," my girlfriend Lynn Santer advised. So, I took her advice and mentioned babies before the first date, of course! Time was running out and I was getting desperate. There was no shortage of men who wanted sex, but it always felt empty and lonely afterwards. And then I gave up. I had this story that all the great guys were taken or gay, so I kept busy with work and thought, "If it's meant to be, it will be." I met this lovely guy, Robert, about 2 years ago. He was like a needle in a haystack, a decent, genuine person, and a gentleman with morals and a great sense of humour.

I liked him but we were both busy and found it challenging to find time to catch up. Then we MADE time and after a few special get-togethers, we realised how much we had in common. Then it happened! We committed to each other and now we're in a relationship!!! I'm 48 and now we're talking babies!! And HE brought it up! It's still possible. Let's see ... what will be will be.

I'm happy with him and happy in my own skin without him too. Together though, we create magic. So grateful for that – and now you know. Here's to more love and less war in the world – however that looks for you.

Starting my business

I started my business AA Xposé Photography in 2002 on the Gold Coast after having a few small car accidents while working late nights with a photography company in Brisbane. After this, I thought, "Why don't I just do this for myself?"

At the time, I was working as a journalist at the Sun Community Newspapers on the Gold Coast. When I left my position at the Sun, the business evolved into AA Xposé Media as people began requesting public relations work, copywriting, video, graphic design, editing and media training services.

I did my first media training workshops in 2003 and had repeated calls for more. In 2014, I launched an online media training program called Mass Media Mastery, where I teach people how to get free publicity and mass media exposure.

I have members of my Mass Media Mastery program and membership site from all over Australia and several countries overseas now, including the Netherlands, South Africa, the US, UK and NZ. Most of them are small business people, authors, speakers, and social entrepreneurs.

Many I have never met in person – such is the power of online marketing! I help people who have a great message, product, or service to share it with the masses using online and offline media so they can build their credibility in the community, business, sales and leave a legacy.

In 2021, I also launched Free Publicity Secrets and Social Media Masterclasses. An advocate for animals and good news, as well as a highly empathic person, I have always had an affinity with animals. After years of seeing animal cruelty and feeling helpless to do anything about it, I founded the world's first Animal Action Day in 2007 to raise awareness, appreciation, and respect for animals. I have since run 15 annual events, raising millions of dollars' worth of free publicity for different animal charities each year.

I have had depression over the years and had four friends take their own lives by the age of 45. As such, I am also passionate about promoting more good news stories in the mass media to help decrease depression and suicide rates worldwide, and lift people's spirits. In line with this, I founded a global Good News Day on August 8, 2018, and the monthly Global Good News Challenge via Facebook Live in June 2020.

A regular Meetup group I run offering marketing advice is Mass Media Tribe and I co-launched the charity Meetup group, The Gold Coast Business Laughter Club, on August 30, 2018.

The elements of my media programs and how they work

In my media training programs, I cover my seven AWESOME steps to gaining free publicity. The AWESOME stands for: A = Articulate Story, W = Work Angles, E = Elevate Profile, S = Startle Media, O = Own Power, M = Master Interviews, E = Explode Impact. I also train clients on social media marketing, including Facebook, Twitter, LinkedIn, Instagram, and YouTube.

For clients who want all their media marketing done for them, I offer Media Star Packages where I uncover the gems of a client's story to develop media angles, press releases, run photo shoots, pitch to the media, follow up with the media and run media training sessions, among other things. I have the only media company I know of that guarantees media exposure.

My goal is to help my clients go from being the world's best kept secret to being a star.

One of my great success stories is from my client Aussie Mega Mall. The directors came to me in 2016 with no media coverage and, after a nationwide PR campaign, we achieved about 40 media spots (including on Channel 7 and Channel 9). This led to them going from having 3000 online stores to 32,000- plus online stores and their business increasing 10-fold in the following 3 years. Now, under the new brand name Explore My Store, they are looking to launch internationally in the US, UK and NZ.

Another one of my clients, Sheila Mac, is a speaker/author of Boot Straps & Bra Straps from Los Angeles. She gained over 50 media appearances in one month in the US and worldwide after she joined my Mass Media Mastery program.

Her Sheila Mac Show on NBC's KCAA radio and on-demand TV gets re-shaped on other platforms and podcast channels and goes out to more than 5 million viewers.

AN EMPOWERED *Life*

Big award win

In late 2021, I was honoured to win the national Bx award for the Print, Media, and Photography category from a field of eight finalists where I was the only female! Across 25 award categories, there were 300 entrants and 180 finalists from Australia and New Zealand.

This was a great honour, particularly as a woman in a male-dominated industry. It shows the divine feminine is rising and is what will bring healing to the planet. My business has tripled through Covid and will continue to grow as I stay true to my mission of inspiring more truth and good news in the media to reduce depression and suicide rates, and lift the consciousness on the planet.

I believe a person on a mission has no competition and there is an abundance of opportunity for everyone.

Ancestral support

I feel a strong drive and support for what I do from my ancestors. Scientifically, it is proven that we carry the DNA of 14 generations.

My great-grandparents were two of the 30,000 Kulaks executed by Stalin's men in the Ukraine in the early 1930s.

As part of the mass eradication of Kulaks as a class, they were hanged outside their house on their farm in Kiev. My grandfather was in another part of the Ukraine at the time and started to speak up about it until his friends said: "Because you're speaking up against the government, they are coming to kill you now." He then ran away to Turkey and met my dad's mum, who was Greek.

I know my ancestors are supporting me spiritually in helping others to stand up in life and speak their truth.

Conscious community global

Lying down on my yoga mat during a quantum DMT breathwork and meditation experience on the Gold Coast in Australia recently, I saw visions of my ancestors and those who have come before me. I couldn't see all their faces, however I recognised their souls. Tears of gratitude and curiosity were flowing down my cheek as I considered what they went through to pave the way for me to be born. I saw a mystical purple haze-like sensation of light flickers flowing towards the right part of my brain – my feminine side – with the message to embrace my feminine side so I could illuminate it and shine brighter for those around me.

Coming out of that experience, I was so inspired to take life to the next level, I created a new Facebook group, titled Conscious Community Global.

The group was created to support and unite conscious communities globally to raise global consciousness to quantum critical mass. One open heart is 5000 times more powerful than a closed mind! It's about being present and loving life regardless of what's happening in the world.

This is a place people can share inspirational photos, quotes, videos and other conscious media to pave the way for a new awakened civilisation. I added links to documentaries and movies that will change lives and potentially save lives. The group now has over 1000 members and continues to grow organically with high engagement.

AN EMPOWERED *Life*

Future goals

I would love to have an offline studio TV show one day – to complement my online shows on the Media Queen TV channel on YouTube.

I love interviewing people and sharing their stories and wisdom. I would also like to start a global movement of more good news stories in the mass media than bad news stories. I believe this will make a massive difference in reducing depression and suicide rates worldwide.

I am passionate about inspiring a positive world where people are optimistic and excited about their lives; a world where people love what they do and are excited about living life to its fullest potential.

I want people to embrace and appreciate the miracle they are as human beings. Just by being born, they have beaten about 1 billion other swimmers to the finish line! Every person is a miracle and has a unique gift and message to bring to the world.

I want to inspire people to recognise and appreciate their gifts, to speak up and speak out about what they are passionate about and for them to create a ripple effect of change by being courageous and speaking their truth honestly and with integrity.

The few who run the world want people to live small lives and be slaves to the system. Many people are brainwashed by the mainstream media and political system, and don't realise they are being brainwashed.

I want people to wake up as individuals and combine forces with other 'awake people' in the community to affect positive change in the world – particularly in the areas of health, peace, sustainability, and environmental protection.

'Question everything!' is my motto. I would also like to set up an animal sanctuary/retreat space to help protect our environment, save endangered animals, and allow people a great space to re-connect with nature.

"Be the change you want to see in the world," as Gandhi said.

And I say: "Shine bright and light up all those around you."

Here's to your success! May you always make the most of every moment in this precious life and live a life which you and your loved ones will be proud of.

CHAPTER 10

Tracey Korman

How I healed my life for my son

This chapter is dedicated to my son.

"Know that YOU are capable of anything you put your mind to!"

Firstly I want to say a warm hello and welcome you to this chapter!

I'm Tracey Korman, also known as the Matchmaking Queen at Two's Company; and a devoted mum to my young adult son, whom I adore.

Most of my childhood years were spent growing up in a country town called Sale in Victoria, Australia. The surrounding area is a beautiful setting of dairy farms and wide open spaces. Simple country town living best describes my childhood living in Sale. My mum had left nursing to be a stay-at-home mum and my father was in the Air force. When I was 6 months old we moved to Penang, Malaysia with the RAAF and enjoyed a really lovely life there; amongst many of my fathers relatives. After 2 years, along with a baby brother, we moved back to Sale where I started primary school. My younger sister was born 2 years later. (According to my mum, I was an easy-going, healthy, well-mannered and well-behaved little girl.) Growing up I joined Brownies and later became a Girl Guide. My brother joined Cubs and played in the Sale soccer team and my sister loved her Callisthenics. We moved to Canberra, ACT (with the RAAF) and continued with our after-school activities including weekly visits to the library to borrow new books. Before relocating back to Sale, we lived in Canberra for 4 years, often enjoying times with cousins who lived there too. Trips to Lakes Entrance and Mallacoota where highlights growing up and a favourite holiday was in Ulladulla, NSW and visiting the snow for my 8th Birthday. My mum always baked, sewed and enjoyed knitting and dad was mostly quiet, conservative and coached my brothers soccer teams. My parents were very organised and life at home was orderly and wholesome.

Rock bottom!........yet again!...

It was a stunning day, blue sky and sunshine and I was sitting in my car with the roof down –(a Saab convertible.) I'd driven into the bottom paddock of the 8 and a half acres I'd bought several years prior, (in Guanaba, the foothills of Mount Tamborine, Gold Coast, Qld, Australia.) Looking up at the very large home on the hill, (which I ended up project managing the building of myself) a home for the family I didn't end up having; double story with a huge balcony surrounded by nature; with a million-dollar nature view. My son was with his dad at the time and this was yet another day where I'd now found myself suicidal. Looking up at that house, clearly my life had hit rock bottom; and there were too many reasons why I didn't want to continue here with my life on earth.

Although I've known beautiful partner love, travelled a lot and seen many of the world's most well known sights, experienced some of life's finest offerings – this was it now – there were too many reasons as mentioned and I was done – it was time for me to go, oh how I so wanted to leave (and end my life.)

My journey included abuse, trauma, loss and betrayal

I survived many suicidal episodes because I have a son who is the light of my life and I could not desert him (fortunately that part of my brain was working where I was not going to leave him behind!!!) Therefore, I had to find a way out of the situation I'd found myself dealing with!!

I scrolled through my phone that day in the car, (seeking inspiration I guess; and feeling desperate) – who could I call and have a chat with? I came across the name of a Personal Development coach Kurek whose programs I'd done; including his fire walk weekend which I'd attended with my precious son (who was 11 at the time.) When speaking with Kurek I shared how I was feeling about my life (I don't recall telling him that I was suicidal – that was something I always kept to myself as a rule!!) Anyway, he asked me what was I grateful for?! I responded, "I'm grateful for my son" ..he then asked what else I was grateful for. This went on for about 15 minutes perhaps, what else was I grateful for?!! He asked me again after I responded, what else I was grateful for?! Thinking of thing's I was grateful for took me out of the space of being suicidal.

Gratitude changed my life that day!!!!

Living with PTSD and clinical depression for 21 years, (diagnosed in 2001) I managed to turn my life around; eventually. For more than a decade few people knew what I was dealing with (smile and no one knows!) It was a long and extremely difficult journey.

My recovery has been a very long process!! Clinical depression is like having to sit in a small closed room and all of the negative thoughts and experiences you've ever had in your life are right there with you in your mind; and you can't escape from them.

The pain of that can be unbearable!! It's like quicksand; feeling like you're sinking and you desperately want to climb out yet you cannot. Our thoughts are extremely powerful – you must know this - the bad ones!! ..and the good ones too!!! I've since learnt that my thinking about the abuse, the extremely unfortunate events that had occurred, the loss, the betrayal – my thinking is what caused the problem! It was my thinking that had me end up suicidal.

Thankfully Gratitude can take you from that space!!...it really can!! These days I refuse to think for too long about any of the events that caused me such pain! Why would I want to do that?!! ...I've plenty to be proud of & I've plenty to be grateful for!

Fast forward and these days, I get to share the wisdom I've learnt with others, like I am sharing with you now! I was so angry one day I could have driven into the closed gates at the entrance to my beautiful acreage property – I wanted to drive straight thru them!!! The anger was immense; that rage was scary! Once passive, I'd become sometimes aggressive – these days I'm a healthy assertive soul which is perfect! Honouring our soul by sharing what doesn't work for us in life means we no longer suppress thoughts and emotions!! .. that's the stuff that can make you sick!!

At some point, in order to survive the emotional pain, I made the decision that gratitude was my go-to!! - It is as simple as that!! Commitment to that decision, as previously mentioned, was life changing!!! I'd realized over time that no one was going to help me, but me!! How could they really?! I allowed music to soothe my soul; I was drawn to listen to beautiful sacred music and also listened to songs loudly in the car like "Born to Live" by Andrea Bocelli and "Shine" by Vanessa Amorosi and "I'm Alive" by Celine Dion. I felt like I was fighting for my life; and it was a battle!! At one point I was struggling to function on a day to day basis – antidepressants enabled me to take care of my son; (and I took very good care of him – always!!) I felt so sad for the things that had happened – the abuse and more, I was surviving day by day – placing one foot in front of the other – I slept for a year. I would be up in the morning with my son for his breakfast, ensure he had everything he needed for the day and then drive him to school. From there I'd drive home, eat some breakfast, set my alarm and then sleep until it was time to go and collect him from school. (To this day I am grateful for the Manageress at the time who was running Two's Company–the Business) I was surviving the situation I'd found myself dealing with.

Many years prior - long ago in fact, I had forgotten me!! – I had disassociated.

Losing my soulmate husband and best friend (he'd lost his way and eventually and suddenly our relationship ended) and in

2007 he passed – I was completely heartbroken. I cried every day for 18 months. Everything else that had occurred didn't compare to losing my best friend.

I lost count the number of times I was suicidal – I had to find a way out!!! ... for my son!!!

These days I feel soft in my heart; (and people had taken advantage of my heart– big time.)

I ask the question ...What makes the future look like a life you want to live into?

Commitment (or lack of) is ALWAYS leading the way!!

Having survived much adversity, (like many others) I know what it takes to dig deep, to do the work that's required and to live the life that I desire!!

I'd grown up being told to think of others before yourself; and for several reasons I'd become a people pleaser. In many ways life had been so unfair (and I'd become stuck in that negative mindset! – every day!!!)

On a positive note - for positive change...

Firstly, I suggest, just begin by making the decision that feeling good is going to be an absolute Priority in your life!! Do all that you can with all that you have to create a life you want to live!!!

AN EMPOWERED *Life*

Overtime, step by step, we can uncover the trauma and pain; and then wisdom appears! ... cool huh?!! ... WOW .... what a journey!!

Step by step we can discover a strength and emotional intelligence that we were not aware existed for us!! With change we grow. Remember the commitment to feeling good? ... that's what will propel you to continue healing! ... one step at a time! Feeling good has to be a priority to living empowered!! Honour YOU! (It can only be from there that we're of benefit to others, in terms of serving or enriching their lives.) Get yourself right and good things will follow; and know what your values are!! Values will act as a light house, guiding you home!!

Personal development

Eventually, I started to rebuild my life one day at a time! I enrolled in courses, programs, and seminars; and I grew; of course! Adversity gifted me with wisdom; and so too has Personal Development!!

These days you'll find pages of inspirational quotes on social media so you can start there if you're new to the personal development journey. Personal growth is an incredible opportunity to become more whole and complete. A sure way to living an Empowered Life is to deal with traumas and pain from the past – while incorporating gratitude into your life daily! Gratitude changed my life remember!! (Gratitude also changes brain chemistry!!)...

In 2012 I became a Qualified Counsellor - (by chance an email had caught my attention.)

I specialise in mental health, trauma, and relationship issues. (Many Two's Company clients benefit greatly from this.) I decided to become a Victor as opposed to a Victim!! Looking back on my childhood, I know I was naïve and gullible, til age 40 years- that cost me dearly in many ways, which is why it's so important that I live my life empowered these days! Losing relationships and real estate (for various reasons, due to villans entering my life) is not something I overcame easily!! These days I like to look forward! (Looking back was incredibly painful I found.)

Despite the negative events from the past, with my beautiful son (who I solely provided private education for and travel abroad) we lived a blessed lifestyle. See the mind can trick you! – for so long I would recall abuse from the past and yet these days if I look back I am learning to remember the beauty instead! The joy, the travel, the longevity of the Business; witnessing my son grow up into a beautiful human being.

I encourage you to look forward and when you do look back my recommendation is that you focus on the positive!! Take the lessons from the past and that's it!!! ..YOU have control over your thoughts - you really do!!! You are the creator of them!!!

That's how to live empowered! ...you know if you look closely, real close, life is very simple really! it's us who complicate it and the quality of our life is a direct proportion to the quality of our thoughts!!! – 100%!!

AN EMPOWERED *Life*

Gratitude and feeling good - a priority in life!! ...

My offering to you is simple – FEEL GOOD...feel healthy, joyful, grateful, and abundant, visualize what you want – NEVER what you don't want – EVER!! ... Along with gratitude (and glutathione) – now usually my life is a breeze!!

When I made the decision that feeling good was an absolute priority in my life – it had to be so!! It was paramount. To live empowered we firstly need to FEEL good!! It took many years, one step at a time - with gratitude as my guiding light; and my son – always my son!

I found something to hold onto, (which was being here for my son!!!) I included gratitude into daily life and made feeling good a priority as I've shared with you. It wasn't a party that's for sure, instead, it was an absolute struggle – I fought for my life; and these days I can feel blessed.

For many years I rocked in a rocking chair on that verandah surrounded by the healing sights and sounds of nature where I would think of things I was grateful for! It is impossible to feel miserable, depressed (or suicidal) and grateful at the same time!! (For 21 years, every year at some point I was suicidal – I had my affairs sorted and a choice of 2 plans to end my life) ..Back to Gratitude!!! ...

I'd play a game with myself where I'd think of 10 things I was grateful for; and then double it! – so YES – now thinking of 20 things I was grateful for!! .. and then 30!! .. If you do that you'll find yourself in a beautiful space of Gratitude! Every time!!!

Tracey Korman

Would you rather be a victim or a victor?

I choose the latter!!! Would you rather feel amazing or mediocre? I taught my son from an early age to think of things he's grateful for and to NEVER think of things he doesn't want as a part of his life experience. How you feel invites more of that feeling into your life! This is a fact and this I have personally experienced. Its law of attraction. If you're feeling happy (and abundant) you'll attract more of both happiness and abundance. If on the other hand you're feeling scarcity and misery well guess what? .. yep - then you'll attract more of that into your life! So go with the flow, think of the life you want, in a direction that serves you!! You can do that!! ..You really can!! – no matter what you've experienced in life!

Affirmations! - Do you know the power of them?! I do!!! They're extremely powerful! For example – "I am happy, healthy and whole, I am living my best life!" Affirmations are a daily part of my life these days and I recommend they be a part of your day too. (Your words AND your thoughts are more powerful than most people realise!!!) Two of the unfortunate events from my past I had once imagined, before they occurred!!

Living life empowered has me feeling good about life and taking responsibility for exactly that! YOU are the answer to how you feel! YOU are the answer to how you live your life! YOU are the creator of living as an empowered being. It all starts with YOU! Being your own best friend – forever and always!! You must be aware of your needs in order to feel good and then of course act on those! No one can treat you better than you because you know how you feel at all times!! Having survived all that took place sees me living my life now very self-aware. If I'm not the best version for me then I am not the best version of me for others!! In 2012 I dedicated my future to my son and

AN EMPOWERED *Life*

my charity goals. I spent a lot of time, for more than 7 years thinking about my son and working on the charity goals. Just last year I realized that although both are extremely dear to my heart, that I really matter too!! Through the continual ongoing personal development and courses, seminars and programs, to relieve me of the emotional pain, trauma and suffering, just like the onion – a layer at a time – my soul is now free, and more alive; and I am now here for me also!!! YAY!! When you step into your life, I mean fully aware and awake as opposed to operating on auto-pilot; you've reached a level that your soul longed for! Ever evolving, ever learning, everlasting!

Having experienced abuse of most kinds and preparing for suicide I now see life through a different lens!! I can easily sit with the broken, the forgotten ones, those feeling abandoned, those suffering with emotional pain and I can offer them my light and some understanding and I encourage them and I like to think that I sprinkle glitter. (I like glitter and I've sat with the homeless.)

I strongly feel that living an empowered life should be taught in schools!!!.. and that gratitude is the gateway and a commitment to yourself to be mindful of how you feel – Everyday!! If you think for a moment of a loved one passed, of course it's very sad that they're no longer here on earth however you are here; and therefore you must be grateful for that gift of your life; if you want to feel empowered! Just like an athlete, it takes daily commitment, every hour of every day! Refuse anything that insults your soul!! Who wants to win at life? ... you do!!! Refuse to accept other people's version of your reality. Move away from what doesn't feel good (unless you're working on healing of course) If you want to feel better than you currently do, then make the decision now for that to happen!! Perhaps have the ring tone of the song "I feel good" as your mobile ring tone! (by musician James Brown.)

Give up any angst, give up any sadness and make the commitment to yourself - anyone can do that if they try hard enough - you can do that NOW!! ... it's up to you, remember! Taking ownership of my life; and years later taking ownership of where things were at, including taking ownership of the adversity ..(it can be a tough believe me!) yet when you do that, when you take ownership you become FREE!!! When we no longer focus on mistakes and how people harmed us for example, rather focus on where we're going; being mindful of what we've learnt from the past, now we're in the driver's seat of our journey!! .. and that's where you want to be!!! .. in the driver's seat of your own life! Your life is right now!!! This very moment is your life!! Precious; and creative! I encourage you to savour peaceful and joyful moments, if you don't already, it's a very beautiful thing to do!! Learn to truly appreciate such moments! Making time to relax and rest will bring them into your life experience.

Allow praise for yourself too!! ... (not just for others!) ...

Embracing Gratitude and while you're at, uplifting music, time with nature and movement are all life giving. Be present and be aware. Create balance in your life!! - or you may find you'll be forced to! Allow for stillness. ..be still, be calm – did you know that calmness is a super power?! (find ways to be calm, meditation is a great place to begin!!) Enjoy the little things in your life. Enjoy moments of stillness, and remember to dream.

Having goals leads you forward and enables you to have the things you want in your life, yet always remember to make time also to enjoy your journey! Take time to FEEL life ...(the healing is in the feeling!!.. go gently!) Allow time for what often goes unnoticed, watching leaves on a tree swaying gently in a breeze or observing the waves on a beach rolling in. Your mind can be your best friend!! How awesome is that?!!! Learn to feed your mind with good stuff; constantly. Feed it with thoughts of encouragement, thoughts that allow you to feel calm, thoughts that have you feeling good!! You've got to say NO MORE to anything other than that!!

I'm here to tell you that YOU can be the hero in your life! You really can. Let go of what doesn't serve you! YOU are the creator of your life experience and everything you need is within You; and coming from You!! Spend time getting to know you more! Don't be afraid to be with yourself, so many people over commit to things, life, people, events etc and there's no room left to be with themselves! Becoming your own best friend you'll make time for you, you'll make time for balance in your life or to do more of the things that you enjoy doing! When I became my own best friend it was a comforting life changing experience; and if you become your own best friend you will experience the same!! (I'm not talking from an ego point of view, I'm talking of a soul level best friend, truly, deeply.)

This year ...2022

In January an RTT (Rapid Therapy Transformation) session proved to be very powerful and I was now determined that I would regain myself – completely!!! - to be living fulfilled and authentically, (without what had become maintenance anti-depressant)– I didn't want that for me! .. I wanted to be completely FREE!! ... and I did it!!!

*(PLEASE NOTE!! – reducing anti-depressants MUST be done gradually!!)

These days I am living with what I describe as a beautiful calmness in my heart, (the rage has long gone; and I am at peace with where I'm at; and I have accepted the past.) I have made peace with my journey and the future is very bright! The personal development journey began the healing!!! For the most part I am healed of the deepest wounds – the ones that affected the core of who I am! Remember that promise I made to be my best friend!!! I will ALWAYS honour me now when it most matters. Dancing, time in the garden sunshine, days on the beach, being with my son, visits to waterfalls, sunsets, relaxing days at home, trips away, live music, taking care of Business - Twos Company (1 year into a 5 year plan) and creating the sustainable future that I want to live is mostly what I do with my time.

Making a difference..

Effortlessly I also get to make a difference in the lives of others. Overcoming the adversity grants me with wisdom and a solid platform upon which to create my future! Rock solid – living from a place of self-care and joy! A commitment to living your life with joy has to be priority when you want a joyous empowered life experience; and you want that, right?! You don't half bake a cake – so don't half do life. Did you know that Joy is your birthright?! Smile... smile right now. Go on, smile! Can you feel yourself relax? Smile some more! – you're feeling lighter right now – your brain is releasing feel good chemicals - as simple as that!! (I was in so much emotional pain in the past that I'd smile while falling asleep – I couldn't bare not to.) .. I'm smiling right now... Aaaah! empowered living... wellbeing... self love!!

AN EMPOWERED *Life*

It's important to remember that the past is not the direction in which you're headed!! (So go ahead and create a life you want to live, one you want to enjoy!!) Life grows to its fullest potential in the present moment! In the present moment we are most in touch with who we are! From there we get to be our most powerful and most authentic. So enjoy!

These days the Business Two's Company is thriving again. (When diagnosed with PTSD and clinical depression in 2002, I stepped away from the Business for several years.) By 2008 I was back in the office Consulting – I down sized the Business and worked part time only – (as was always intended actually.) I won't grow the Business again myself (once a Team of 13 and annually $7 figures) however I know that someone else out there may like to do that and I am open for that person / people to show up in my life. The office is busy.

In the mean-time, I feel very blessed to still enjoy Matchmaking, along with providing dating & relationship coaching, personal development through our Programs at Two's Company. Our clients are singles seeking long term companionship or marriage / long term partner - ages 18 years to 89! (In 1990 I'd returned from living in London where I'd been based for 2 years) and I ended up working for an Introduction service in Melbourne - had moved there with family at age 13yrs.) I later discovered the company I was working for weren't' looking after their clients as they should have! (I was also brought up with the saying "do unto others as you would have them do unto you" aka The Golden Rule.) I enjoyed matchmaking, was good at it too and so the idea for Two's Company came to me. By October 1995 I'd moved to the beautiful sunny Gold Coast Queensland (for the climate) and Two's Company began operating. I was a Co Founder and referrals quickly became a common thing and still are to this day – now 27 years later. I've had more success for my clients than in my own personal love journey and you know what that means?.. it means that I understand my clients extremely well. (It also means that I still may have true lasting love for me someday.)

In closing, I know that what I've shared with you will absolutely enhance many lives and that gives me great joy!

Decide, commit to YOU, have gratitude and make Feeling good a Priority! We are a focusing mechanism, so focus on what you want!!

My parting gift for you ....(there are several) ..

- If you want to Look, Live OR Feel your absolute best then you really can!

- Remember Gratitude, Present moments, Music, Movement, Stillness and Feeling good!

- I Highly recommend the following amazing products ...

  The key word is Glutathione!! (prices are in US dollars.) For information visit https://www.neumi.com/traceyk/

- (Business opportunities are also available for anyone seeking additional income - my office direct line = 0405 536 155)

- For anyone struggling with overcoming abuse or depression an interview is available on UTUBE – when I first spoke publicly about most of the events from my past – (Media Queen interviews Tracey Korman.) P.S Trigger warning and correction – instead of don't watch the TV I meant to say don't watch the news!!!

"Be gentle with you! ...real gentle!!
Commit and let it be so!!! ....
Fall in love with YOU and your life!! ......
Be the Victor – NOT the Victim!!
Recover and reclaim!!!
Empowering thoughts are essential to living an empowered life ... your thoughts have power!!!
Constantly ever evolving, ever learning, everlasting."

Authors Biographies

AA Xposé Media

Known as the Media Queen, Aldwyn Altuney is a photojournalist with 38 years' experience in TV, radio, print and online media.

Aldwyn hosts Media Queen TV – Inspiring Truth and Good News on YouTube and for 3 years, co-hosted the Techwebcast podcast, which had over 1 million downloads in 8 years.

Born in Sydney and based on the Gold Coast since 2000, Aldwyn runs AA Xposé Media, which offers public relations, photography and videography services plus the worldwide Mass Media Mastery training program.

Passionate about raising awareness, appreciation and respect for animals, she founded the world's first Animal Action Day in 2007.

She has since run 15 annual events, raising millions of dollars' worth of free publicity for different animal charities each year.

Passionate about promoting more good news stories in the mass media to help decrease depression and suicide rates worldwide and lift people's spirits, Aldwyn founded a Global Good News Day on August 8, 2018, and the monthly Global Good News Challenge in June 2020.

Meetup groups she has run since 2018 are Mass Media Tribe and The Gold Coast Business Laughter Club.

She has featured in 15 inspiring compilation books, many of which are international best-sellers.

As a reporter on TV, radio and print media globally for over 30 years, she has interviewed stars including Charlie Sheen, Hugh Jackman, Russell Crowe and Cyndi Lauper.

She also loves performing in her comedy duo The Fiddly Gigglers, acting, playing ukulele, beach walks and body surfing.

Connect: www.linktr.ee/aldwyn

Christine Innes

The Corporate Escapists

Christine Innes is a Coach, Speaker, #1 International Best Seller Author, host of The Corporate Escapists Podcast, and editor-in-chief of The Corporate Escapists Magazine.

Christine is the CEO and Founder of The Corporate Escapists, a global company empowering people to transform their lives by letting go of their corporate identity and finding and following their passion.

Christine's clients say:

"I have been lucky to be featured in the magazine, however, what I cherished the most is that Christine has held my hand through the process of rebranding. I love it! I highly recommend anyone wishing to have a fabulous take in a new direction to call Christine, she is a champion through and through." - Dr. Anne-Marie

"Christine has been our business coach at Curious Me for several months. Wow, what a difference one-on-one coaching makes! Christine gave us the inspiration, motivation, and accountability we needed to go from planning for the now, to see the future. We started setting ourselves serious business goals and with her help, put in place action plans and timelines to make it happen. We experienced our best financial quarter EVER, even with COVID interruptions. all thanks to her help. We are forever grateful for Christine, her support, mentorship, and friendship." - Curious Me

Christine is passionate about helping people be themselves and create a life they love.

Christine offers 1:1 coaching with her two signature programs:

EmpowHER: A 12-week program helping you go from corporate mess to your empowHERed best

The Corporate Kickoff Program: A 60-day program to launch your business online.

Facebook: @christineinnescoach @thecorporateescapists
Instagram: @christine_innes @thecorporateescapists
Website: www.thecorporateescapists.com

Jenell Kelly

CEO Aligned Life

With 30 years in the field of nursing and recognized as the 26th International Top Achiever in her NWM direct sales company, Wellness Expert Jenell Kelly enthusiastically leads her clients to next levels of performance. As a Leadership Success Trainer, Amazon #1 International Best-Selling Author, Keynote Speaker, and Certified Clarity Catalyst Coach she provides inspiration and tools for success. Her background in healthcare and leadership expands over several industries including management, sales, and education. Jenell worked her way up from an entry level position to now being the owner and CEO of Aligned Life, and Founder of the You-GLOW-Girl Women's Empowerment Community.

Website: jenelllyn.com
Linktree: linktr.ee/Jenelllyn

Kleo Merrick

Merrick Courses Pty Ltd

Kleo Merrick is an International Bestselling Author, Speaker, and Marketing Strategist.

Kleo is the CEO of Merrick Courses, a company she founded in 2013 where she runs successful Workshops, Online Training Programs and teaches businesses how to market their services with Sales Funnels, Webinars and Online Courses. And educates them on how to manoeuvre Digital Marketing specifically for Entrepreneurs.

Her clients say: "Kleo taught me more in 2 hours than it would have taken me 5 years to learn myself…!!!" – Cathy Kingsley

She is the author of: ~ 'An Inspired Life: 10 inspirational stories from women around the world who have dared to follow their passion', 'I Did It: 16 Mindset Secrets To Transform The Life You Have Into The Ultimate Life you Desire', 'Yes I Can: 16 Success Secrets Form Inspiring Women Around The World', and 'Compelling Selling: How To Earn More By Selling Less'.

'Entrepreneurs Academy' - Online Business School focused on supporting Small Business Owners with Entrepreneurial Business Skills. 'Online Course Academy' – 6-week Online Program How to Create & Sell your 1st Online Course. 'Accelerated Webinar Program' – 6-week Online Program to create Webinars Simply and Easily from scratch, without any of the Techy Jargon. 'Online Course Mastery Program' – 12-Month Mentoring Program to Convert your current Knowledge into Tangible, Saleable & Irresistible Online Content on Autopilot.

Kleo is extremely passionate about Creating a Community of Passionate Business Owners and Upskilling them in the Digital World.

Email: kleo@kleomerrick.com
Facebook: www.facebook.com/marketingwithkleo/
Instagram: www.instagram.com/kleomerrick/
LinkedIn: www.linkedin.com/in/kleomerrick/

Kylie James

Kylie James Coaching

Kylie James is a Transition Coach and Mentor, People Strategist, International Bestselling Author, and Speaker.

Kylie is the founder of Kylie James Coaching. She combines her experience in the fields of leadership, human resource management and coaching to help individuals, teams and organisations to increase their confidence so they feel valued, heard and seen. Her mission is to inspire people to stop seeking out mediocre and aim for excellence no matter what their role in life is.

Kylie has three main ways you can connect and work with her:

- **Inspiring Change Program** - Coaching and mentoring tailored to the individual or group
- **Nine to Thrive Corporate Coaching** - This allows leaders to take a step back, look at the bigger picture and discover what changes might be needed to successfully create and lead a positive and inclusive team environment and culture where individuals can thrive.
- **The Mid-Life Mayhem and Magic Community** - A Facebook community where women who are either approaching or in their mid-lives can come together and support each other through this phase of life.

Website: www.kyliejamescoaching.com.au
Email: hello@kyliejamescoaching.com.au
Facebook: www.facebook.com/kyliejamescoaching
FB Group: www.fb.com/groups/midlifemayhemandmagic/
Instagram: www.instagram.com/kyliejamescoaching
LinkedIn: www.linkedin.com/in/kylie-james-cphr-6a066b20

Lisa Ohtaras

Caring Energetic Healing

Lisa Ohtaras is a Best Selling Author, renowned Energy Healer, Soul Healer, Intuitive Spiritual Coach, Spiritual Educator, Reiki Master, Seichim Master, Medium, Channel, Soulful Forgiveness & Self Forgiveness/Self-Acceptance & Atonement Practitioner & Workshop Facilitator.

Over two and a half decades ago, Lisa healed herself of Multiple Sclerosis (M.S.) warning signs. Her diagnosis initiated an awakening from her spiritual slumber and connected Lisa to her inner self.

Lisa transformed pain, numbness alternating with pins and needles in her hands and arms, feet and limbs, night sweats, insomnia, chronic fatigue, and visual challenges, all without medication.

Through her Spiritual connection, consistent daily meditation, personal growth, Spiritual growth and development, Lisa restored balance, harmony, and well-being to her physical body and emotional state.

Following Lisa's self-healing, she continued to work in her nursing career which collectively spanned over two decades. Then in 2003, Lisa commenced living her Soul Purpose Sacred Contract and has been helping people with physical and life challenges, emotional matters of the heart and forgiveness challenges to live in balance, harmony, health, and the greatest version of themselves.

Website: www.caringenergetichealing.com
Facebook: www.facebook.com/lisaohtaras
Instagram: www.instagram.com/lisaohtaras
Linkedin: www.linkedin.com/in/lisaohtaras

Marika Gare

Perth Virtual Services

Marika Gare is an international best-selling author, international multi-award winner, Business Operational Management Specialist, Mentor, and Women's Circle Facilitator. She grew up in Perth, Western Australia, and is the mother to a beautiful boy.

Marika is also the founder and Director of Perth Virtual Services, a company founded in 2019 that provides operational management support to small and medium businesses together with intuitive business mentoring to provide business owners with the right tools to align and succeed in their business.

Marika is very passionate about encouraging and empowering other women to ignite their dreams and follow their hearts. She provides mentoring and support to women, providing tools to follow their own inner compass and embrace life through all the challenges.

Website: www.perthvirtualservices.com.au
Email: admin@perthvirtualservices.com.au
Facebook: www.facebook.com/perthvirtualservices
Instagram: www.instagram.com/perthvirtualservices
LinkedIn: www.linkedin.com/in/marikagare

Terri Tonkin

Connect Within

Terri is a multiple International Best-Selling author; ghostwriter, speaker; facilitator; mentor and coach. Her own book, My Time To Shine, started her love and passion for writing. She has been a contributor to several compilation books, and has recently expanded her writing passion by offering ghostwriting services for those wishing to tell their stories.

She is the face of Connect Within, and her clients are heard, validated, acknowledged, encouraged and supported to find the solutions they are searching for.

Terri aspires to inspire the people she meets to reach their potential, as inspiration leads to motivation, and motivation leads to action, providing results.

Her life has been a journey of ups and downs, trials and tribulations, both personally and professionally. She is a life-long learner, seeks out new opportunities, is an avid reader and loves to travel.

Facebook: www.facebook.com/connectwithinmindsetlifecoach/
Email: terri@connectwithin.com.au
LinkedIn: www.linkedin.com/in/terri-tonkin/
Website: www.connectwithin.com.au

Tracey Korman

Twos Company - Matchmaking

Tracey Korman is a Co Founder of Twos Company – Matchmaking.

Australia wide Matchmaking Service - www.twoscompany.com.au

Tracey is known as 'The Matchmaking Queen'

She is a Qualified Counsellor – specialising in mental health, trauma and relationship issues.

Featured in International womens day calendar - Gold Coast - 2016

Is a committed participant of The Vinnies CEO sleepout.

Is a Founding Member of Animal action events - raising awareness, appreciation and respect for animals.

Is a Committee Member and Volunteer of Gold Coast Community Christmas lunch.

Tracey is passionate about: Helping singles find love long term ....seeing Truth and Justice in the world ... Helping the homeless and causes for them.... Supporting child protection causes .... and helping people overcome adversity and create a life they want to live.

She loves to dance whenever possible and is committed to having a healthy life balance.

Connect: 0405 536 155
Web: www.twoscompany.com.au

Vallye Adams
Etavele Solutions

Vallye Adams is the founder and CEO of Etavele Solutions, LLC, a national consulting firm based in Tampa Florida. Unique like her name, Etavele offers solutions to 'elevate' and enhance events, engage boards, specializing in proven sustainable revenue development in the not for profit sector.

After attending the University of South Florida, Vallye's professional experience spans over twenty five years, including multifamily property management, real estate sales, and over twelve years in executive nonprofit management, fundraising, event development, expansion strategies and new market growth.

Her "WOO" (Winning others Over) strength and collaborative style has cultivated relationships, sponsorships and corporate partnerships, paving the way for organizations around the country to elevate revenue and enhance event fundraising. Vallye's ability to help sail these vital "ships" has elevated organizations revenue growth over $20 million in the last 5 years. Experienced in expansion initiatives and new market growth in 22 states, Vallye focuses on grassroots efforts, building cohesive teams, motivated volunteers, and active structured boards.

Vallye believes actions speak louder than words and offers to personally help your organization make "the ask" and show you the money $$! She is a licensed auctioneer in multiple states and event emcee with the incredible team at Alpert Enterprises! She offers to consult and coach clients on cultivating exceptional events and actually facilitate, manage and lead the revenue appeal from the frontlines....the stage!

Website:	www.etavelesolutions.com
Email:	vallye@etavelesolutions.com
Facebook:	www.facebook.com/etavelesolutions/
Instagram:	@etavelesolutions
LinkedIn:	www.linkedin.com/company/etavele-solutions/

www.ingramcontent.com/pod-product-compliance
Lightning Source LLC
Chambersburg PA
CBHW041142110526
44590CB00027B/4103